EVALUATING BOARDS AND ADMINISTRATORS

EVALUATING BOARDS AND ADMINISTRATORS

Promoting Greater Accountability in Higher Education

Jeffrey L. Buller

ROWMAN & LITTLEFIELD
Lanham • Boulder • New York • London

Published by Rowman & Littlefield
An imprint of The Rowman & Littlefield Publishing Group, Inc.
4501 Forbes Boulevard, Suite 200, Lanham, Maryland 20706
www.rowman.com

6 Tinworth Street, London SE11 5AL, United Kingdom

Copyright © 2021 by Jeffrey L. Buller

All rights reserved. No part of this book may be reproduced in any form or by any electronic or mechanical means, including information storage and retrieval systems, without written permission from the publisher, except by a reviewer who may quote passages in a review.

British Library Cataloguing in Publication Information Available

Library of Congress Cataloging-in-Publication Data

Names: Buller, Jeffrey L., author.
Title: Evaluating boards and administrators : promoting greater accountability in higher education / Jeffrey L. Buller.
Description: Lanham : Rowman & Littlefield, [2020] | Includes bibliographical references and index. | Summary: "By combining recent research in how performance is actually improved in corporate organizations with best practices at existing colleges and universities, this book provides a practical system that institutions can adapt for evaluating their governing boards and administrators"— Provided by publisher.
Identifiers: LCCN 2020009838 (print) | LCCN 2020009839 (ebook) | ISBN 9781475854763 (cloth) | ISBN 9781475854770 (paperback) | ISBN 9781475854787 (epub)
Subjects: LCSH: Educational accountability. | Education, Higher—Administration—Evaluation. | Universities and colleges—Administration. | College trustees.
Classification: LCC LB2806.22 .B85 2020 (print) | LCC LB2806.22 (ebook) | DDC 379.1/58—dc23
LC record available at https://lccn.loc.gov/2020009838
LC ebook record available at https://lccn.loc.gov/2020009839

To the memory of John Pritchett (1942–2018), provost and interim president at Florida Atlantic University and acting/interim provost and vice president for academic affairs at Auburn University.

CONTENTS

Preface ix
Introduction xiii

1 Evaluation and the Accountability Culture 1
2 How to Evaluate Administrators Effectively 33
3 Best Practices in Administrative Evaluations 61
4 How to Evaluate Boards Effectively 85
5 Best Practices in Board Evaluations 115
6 Putting It All Together: Developing Synergy in Assessment, Program Review, Accreditation, and Evaluation 143

Other Books by Jeffrey L. Buller 161
More about ATLAS 163
Index 167
About the Author 173

PREFACE

Colleges and universities have always believed in the practice of objective and thorough evaluation. They evaluate their students from the very moment they arrive in order to assign them to the right level of courses, and they evaluate their students before they leave in order to determine whether they've met all the requirements for their degrees.

They evaluate faculty members through student ratings of instruction, peer reviews, promotion and tenure reviews, and post-tenure reviews. They evaluate staff members through regular performance appraisals. They evaluate courses through outcomes assessment. They even evaluate entire programs and offices through periodic program reviews.

So, why aren't administrators and boards expected to undergo this same type of objective and thorough evaluation?

Many administrators and board members will argue that they are, in fact, evaluated regularly. Presidents or chancellors frequently submit themselves to evaluation by their governing boards, and these boards may conduct their own annual self-evaluations.

But self-evaluation or evaluation only by one's direct supervisors is totally different from the type of intense, 360-degree evaluation that faculty members and even some members of the staff experience, and it's not nearly as thorough and rigorous as the type of evaluation colleges and universities require of their students.

So, we must ask ourselves again this question: Why aren't administrators and boards expected to undergo the same type of objective and thorough evaluation as other members of the higher education community?

That question has taken on special urgency recently as legislatures have begun demanding increased accountability of senior administrators in light of scandals and the acts of misconduct that have occurred at a number of institutions. For example, at the University of Illinois, the president resigned after it came to light that certain applicants for admission received special consideration solely because of their political connections. A president at American University was forced out after it was revealed that he had used university funds to cover personal expenses. A president of Hillsdale College was asked to resign after it became public that he'd had an improper relationship with his own daughter-in-law.

Governing boards, too, are under greater scrutiny. Several regional accreditors have adopted standards requiring that higher education boards be evaluated. Critics on the right sometimes claim that governing boards are too liberal; critics on the left sometimes claim that governing boards are too conservative. "Who is evaluating the boards that evaluate our senior administrators?" it is asked.

Despite these trends, however, the type of review that most administrators and boards receive is far less stringent than the types of review expected for other members of the college or university. Board and administrative evaluations are usually far too limited in scope and fail to incorporate best practices developed in both the academic and corporate worlds.

This book examines why current approaches to administrative and governing board evaluations are inadequate and how those approaches can and should be improved. It recommends a new approach to these reviews based on current research about how performance appraisals should be conducted, and it summarizes best practices that institutions need to adopt.

Readers will learn why changing the way in which we evaluate board members and administrators is an important component of efforts to improve the quality of higher education. They will learn what to include on evaluation instruments, what not to include, and how the items on these instruments should be phrased.

The goal of this work is to help colleges and universities meet the new requirements imposed by legislatures and accrediting bodies while also designing systems that are not cumbersome to implement or that require the investment of significant time and resources. The author's hope is that an improved approach to the evaluation of administrators and governing boards can become one more tool every school has in its toolkit for serving the needs of its students and community.

INTRODUCTION

Evaluating Boards and Administrators was written in order to provide a concise yet complete description of how presidents, chancellors, provosts, governing boards, and the individual members of those boards should be reviewed as a way of improving their performance. It is structured in such a way as to offer both an ideal to strive for and concrete, practical suggestions that can be implemented immediately.

Chapter 1 presents the case for taking a new look at how senior administrators and governing boards are evaluated. It examines why the issue of evaluation is particularly timely right now and why current systems for conducting these evaluations aren't as effective as they can and should be. Chapter 2 introduces a new approach to evaluating administrators, based on research indicating what works in performance appraisals, what doesn't work, and who should be consulted during the evaluation of any employee's performance, even if that employee is the president or chancellor.

Chapter 3 moves from the theoretical to the practical, examining the systems in place at several institutions that can serve as leaders in their approaches to administrative evaluations. It draws lessons from these approaches that other schools can adapt for their own use. Chapter 4 returns to a more research-oriented perspective, examining the shortcomings that can be found in the methods currently used to evaluate governing boards, proposing a vastly improved approach to board evaluation, and making the case that individual board members, not merely the board as a whole, also should be evaluated regularly.

Chapter 5 explores best practices in the corporate and academic worlds that can be implemented at institutions of higher education in order to establish a more objective, thorough, and efficient method of evaluating governing boards. Chapter 6 summarizes the arguments made elsewhere in the book, suggesting a way in which administrative and board evaluation can be aligned with other appraisal processes at the institution, including employee evaluation, outcomes assessment, and program review. It also makes the case that, although the current impetus for the reform of evaluation procedures stems at least in part from the requirements of accrediting bodies, those very requirements have become unwieldy and now need to be reformed both for the sake of better administrative and board evaluations and to improve the quality of higher education generally.

Evaluating Boards and Administrators is intended for a number of different audiences:

- Faculty members and administrators at institutions that are either creating a system of administrative and board evaluation or revising a current system: the book will suggest pitfalls to avoid, model systems to strive for, and best practices to imitate.
- Representatives and employees of accrediting bodies, whether regional or devoted to a specific academic program, who are looking for guidance in how to develop standards for administrative and board evaluation and who are seeking to improve the accreditation process generally.
- Students of higher education leadership at both the undergraduate and graduate level who want information about a significant current issue in the governance of colleges and universities and hope to prepare themselves for the challenges they'll face in their professional positions.
- Reading groups at institutions of higher education that are seeking a concise and yet provocative exploration of an issue that affects them directly and about which they can propose new ideas.

- Leadership development programs at colleges and universities that are seeking a resource that takes a "deeper dive" into the topic of fair and effective evaluation.
- Individual readers who want to learn about a topic of great importance in higher education that is frequently given short shrift in books on leadership and management or that is ignored entirely.

Although examples of admirable evaluation policies for administrators and boards exist at many more institutions than can possibly be cited in this book, a significant number of those policies are outlined in documents available to that institution's internal community only and thus not accessible to the reader. Since readers may want to explore additional aspects of these policies on their own, preference has been given to institutions that make their procedures open and readily accessible to the public.

I'd like to thank editorial assistant, Rebecca Peter, for her contributions to an early version of this manuscript; my editor at Rowman & Littlefield, Tom Koerner, for his consistent support throughout this and many other projects; and all those institutions mentioned in the pages that follow for providing excellent examples for the rest of us to follow.

Jeffrey L. Buller
Raleigh, North Carolina
March 15, 2020

I

EVALUATION AND THE ACCOUNTABILITY CULTURE

For much of their history, institutions of higher education operated with a great degree of autonomy. Courts of law, particularly in the United States, were hesitant to intervene in such matters as admission policies, grading standards, and course content, believing that the colleges and universities themselves were best equipped to make decisions about who should be taught in these schools, what they should learn there, and how the faculty should be hired and evaluated.

At major, internationally acclaimed universities like Oxford and Cambridge, the view was that society as a whole benefited from allowing scholars to pursue their inquiries without much government interference since today's "pure research" might well serve as the basis for tomorrow's "applied technology," and politicians didn't regard themselves as appropriately trained to make decisions that were best left to experts in their field.

Even those who were funding education and research at colleges and universities—legislatures, educational boards, parents, and students themselves—were content to allow decisions about what was studied and how it was studied to professors and administrators.

This laissez faire approach to higher education began to change—slowly at first but then with increasing rapidity—following World War II and the passage of the GI Bill in the United States.

Once a university education shifted from being an opportunity for only the "best and brightest" (which largely consisted of students who were both gifted enough to benefit from the experience and wealthy enough to afford it) to being an instrument of social mobility and a pathway to the middle class, the question of *how well schools were doing* at fulfilling their missions was routinely asked. The accountability culture was born.

Today at a college or university, everyone seems to be evaluating everyone else. Faculty members grade their students, and students complete course evaluations about the faculty members. Chairs evaluate faculty members, and faculty members evaluate their chairs. Deans appraise the performance of their chairs, and chairs appraise the performance of their deans.

This type of universal mutual evaluation has both advantages and disadvantages. On the positive side, it makes it possible to form a far clearer picture of each person's performance because the institution receives data, not merely from the level above that person, but from all dimensions: superiors, peers, and direct reports.

A system of comprehensive appraisal—commonly referred to as a *360-degree evaluation*—can a valuable tool in helping people improve their performance. It takes into account the people who are affected by a decision as well as the perspectives of colleagues who have to make similar decisions and allows supervisors to interpret behaviors in a larger context.

As Katie Conboy, provost and senior vice president at Simmons University in Boston, says, 360-degree evaluation is particularly important for "middle managers" in higher education.

> Deans are in an interesting spot—in one sense they are the CEOs [chief executive officers] of their unit, and in another they're middle managers of the university. . . . So they need to hear from those who see them as their CEO and also from people who see them as partners. I think that's a helpful balancing. (Tugend, 2019)

But what if the group being evaluated doesn't consist of "middle managers"? What if there's a need to evaluate an institution's governing board, a body that often occupies the *highest* level in the institutional hierarchy? Since there's no supervisory rank *above* the board, genuine 360-degree evaluation isn't possible. So, what's the best way in which to evaluate a governing board?

Some systems will argue that this issue really doesn't exist because there *is* a supervisory level above the governing board, namely the governor or legislature. In some cases, too, a system-wide president or chancellor presides over the governing boards of member institutions and can serve as the supervisor who participates in the board's 360-degree evaluation.

But these answers merely shift the problem up one more level on the organizational chart. Eventually, as you move up the ranks in any hierarchy, you reach the highest level which, by definition, doesn't report to anyone else. Who evaluates *them*? Or in the words of the satirist Juvenal, *Quis custodiet ipsos custodes?* ("Who will guard the guards themselves?" 6.347–348).

MANDATES FOR ACCOUNTABILITY

These questions are not merely theoretical in nature. There is a growing mandate that *all* levels of institutions and systems in higher education be accountable for demonstrating that they're achieving their goals and serving as effective stewards of the resources entrusted to them.

For example, Standard 3.8 of the New England Commission of Higher Education requires that

> The board systematically develops, ensures, and enhances its own effectiveness through orientation, professional development, and *periodic evaluation*. Its role and functions are effectively carried out through appropriate committees and meetings. (emphasis added; Standards for Accreditation, 2016)

The implication of this standard is that the board will evaluate itself. But other accrediting bodies go even further in specifying that a procedure for self-evaluation by the governing board is required.

In its section on board and administrative organization, the Accrediting Commission for Community and Junior Colleges of the Western Association of Schools and Colleges mandates that "The governing board's *self-evaluation processes* for assessing board performance are clearly defined, implemented, and published in its policies or bylaws" (Accreditation Standards, 2012).

Standard 2.A.8 of the Northwest Commission on Colleges and Universities states that, in order to qualify for accediation, it's required that the governing board of an institution "regularly *evaluates its performance* to ensure its duties and responsibilities are fulfilled in an effective and efficient manner" (NWCCU Standards, 2019).

In much the same way, Standard 4.2.g of the Southern Association of Colleges and Schools Commission on Colleges (SACSCOC) requires that "The governing board defines and regularly evaluates its responsibilities and expectations" (Principles of Accreditation, 2018).

On the surface, the SACSCOC requirement appears to be quite narrow in focus: all that governing boards need to do in their self-evaluation is to examine their "responsibilities and expectations." But the "Questions to Consider" section of the *Resource Manual* provided to institutions during the accreditation or reaffirmation process suggests that the scope of the board's self-evaluation should be quite broad indeed.

- What are the legal obligations of board members? Does each member of the board understand these expectations?
- Do bylaws and other written documents for board procedures make clear the role of and limits of board actions?
- Do bylaws and other written documents for the board distinguish the roles between the board (policy making) and the CEO (administrative)?
- Is the board structure working well? Are committee responsibilities well defined?

- Is the orientation of new board members effective?
- How does the board stay informed as to the financial health of the institution?
- How does the board maintain its focus on the institutional mission?
- Is review of the mission statement a regular expectation of the governing board?
- What is the relationship between the institution's chief executive officer and the institution's governing board?
- What protections are built into the board structure to ensure the board is not subject to undue influence by a minority of members or by external forces?
- Are board minutes clear and accurate? Do they provide sufficient detail to capture the results of deliberations?
- Do board procedures regarding protection from internal conflicts of interest work appropriately?
- Does the board have a functioning self-evaluation process?
- Are procedures for CEO succession clear?
- If the governing board interacts with other boards (e.g., system boards, foundation boards, alumni boards), are duties and expectations clear? (Resource Manual for the Principles of Accreditation, 2018)

Requiring the self-evaluation of governing boards is clearly a trend among accreditation bodies in higher education. Even for institutions where such an evaluation process is not currently compulsory, administrators and board members may expect that such a standard will be adopted in the near future.

Even today, however, it's nearly a universal requirement among accrediting bodies that the institution's CEO be evaluated. Accreditation by the Middle States Commission on Higher Education requires that the school's CEO be "appointed by, evaluated by, and reports to the governing body" (Standards for Accreditation and Requirements of Affiliation, 2019).

Standard 2.A.7 of the Northwest Commission on Colleges and Universities states that "The board selects and evaluates regularly a chief executive officer who is accountable for the operation of the institution" (NWCCU Standards, 2019). And Standard 4.2.c of the Southern Association of Colleges and Schools Commission on Colleges mandates that "The governing board selects and regularly evaluates the institution's chief executive officer" (Principles of Accreditation, 2018).

POTENTIAL PROBLEMS WITH EVALUATING BOARD AND ADMINISTRATORS

But there are potential (and sometimes *actual*) problems with these requirements. To begin with, in the case of board evaluation, can any system that begins and ends with self-evaluation be truly thorough and effective? Certainly, self-evaluation is a valuable component of any 360-degree evaluation system, but is it sufficient by itself?

The evidence would suggest that it's not. As one review of the literature on self-assessments has concluded,

> The correlation between self-ratings of skill and actual performance in many domains is moderate to meager—indeed, at times, other people's predictions of a person's outcomes prove more accurate than that person's self-predictions. . . . Complete strangers armed only with scant information about an individual can predict that person's skills and abilities almost as well as he or she can, despite the fact that the individual has a lifetime of self-information to draw upon. (Dunning, Heath, & Suls, 2004, 69, 71)

In self-evaluations, people tend to either overestimate their success or undervalue their accomplishments out of a sense of modesty. The highly nuanced view of a person or group's performance that is obtained by a 360-degree evaluation is rarely obtained through self-appraisal.

In a similar way, certain problems result from the requirement that the *governing board* be the group responsible for the evaluation of the CEO. Members of the governing board—often referred to as a board of regents, trustees, or visitors—typically come from fields outside of higher education and may assume that the way in which successful leadership is demonstrated in their own organization is the way it's best demonstrated at a college or university.

> Members of a governing board are probably more at home in hierarchical organizations than distributed, decentralized or modified-matrix styles of decision making [such as those found in higher education]. For this reason, they may be frustrated or confused when they learn that a department chair or dean cannot simply order a faculty member to do certain things. Concepts like tenure and academic freedom may be foreign to them, or they may have distorted ideas about what these terms mean. They may think that tenure means a faculty member can't be fired for any reason, or that academic freedom means that professors can do or say whatever they want in their classrooms. Their only experience of a college or university is likely to have been as a student, and students see the institution very differently from those employed there. (Buller & Reeves, 2018, p. 87)

Based on these assumptions, members of a governing board may assume that a president or chancellor isn't being effective because he or she isn't leading in the manner that someone in the corporate, legislative, or military worlds would lead. A 360-degree evaluation might provide a corrective to that assumption, but, if that type of evaluation isn't specifically required, it isn't likely to be done.

In addition to these issues, there are many other challenges that must be addressed if administrators and governing boards are to be evaluated fairly, accurately, and effectively.

First, performance reviews of any kind have a demonstrably poor track record of actually achieving their fundamental purpose: improving people's performance. Adobe, the maker of the popular software packages Photoshop and Creative Cloud, completely eliminated traditional performance reviews after finding that they were considered "unproductive and irrelevant by employees and their managers who go through them" (Rodriguez, 2017).

Why doesn't the evaluation process work the way in which it is supposed to? To begin with, the evaluations are extremely time consuming. Rather than doing their actual work, both managers and employees devote long hours—Adobe's research estimated roughly seventeen hours per employee—on a process that "office workers feel . . . [has] no impact on how they do their job (59 percent) and . . . [is] a needless HR requirement (58 percent)" (Rodriguez, 2017).

In addition, the study concluded that

> Structured performance reviews can elicit dramatic reactions, as rankings and ratings create competition and breed stress. More than half of office workers agree that performance reviews put them in competition with one another (57 percent), and their manager plays favorites (61 percent). (Rodriguez, 2017)

Researchers confirmed Adobe's findings and cited other reasons why performance evaluations typically failed to improve performance. A study conducted by psychologists at Kansas State University, Eastern Kentucky University, and Texas A&M University reproduced a finding that will be familiar to any college professor who ever tried to increase student motivation by practicing "tough love" and assigning very low grades in an effort to "spur" performance.

People who are already trying hard tend to internalize negative observations about their performance, react badly to criticism, and do less well in the future; people who aren't putting in much effort tend to blame the reviewer for negative observations, remain indifferent to criticism, and not try any harder in the future (Culbertson, Henning, & Payne, 2013). As a result, nearly a third of performance reviews ended up actually causing a decline in employee performance (Kluger & DeNisi, 1996).

Second, it's not often clear that evaluation systems accurately evaluate what they claim to evaluate. For example, to shift from employee appraisals to college student course evaluations for a moment, there are a number of studies that suggest professors who offer easier grades and a lighter workload received higher ratings than did professors who were tougher graders and more demanding in the work they assigned (d'Apollonia & Abrami, 1997; Eiszler, 2002; Germain & Scandura, 2005; Griffin, 2004).

Some observers counter, however, that there are also several studies suggesting that there is little or no correlation between student ratings of instruction and the grades or workload assigned in the course (Aruyabi & Delta State University, 2003; Gravestock & Gregor-Greenleaf, 2008; Marsh & Roche 2000). At the present time, the issue is best regarded as unresolved.

Nevertheless, even the persistence of this debate raises serious questions about *what it is that student course evaluations really evaluate*. They certainly don't measure the effectiveness of a professor's teaching since they make no effort at all to determine what a student has learned.

In many ways, therefore, course evaluations aren't much different from *satisfaction surveys* that report the degree to which students enjoyed a course and the professor's style in conducting it. Other factors may also contribute to the scores on student course evaluations: the size of the class, whether the course is an elective or required, the time of day at which the course was taught or when the evaluation was conducted, and the age, ethnicity, and gender of the professor.

Certainly, an impressive body of research has indicated that the way in which faculty evaluations are conducted in higher education results in a bias against female professors (Basow & Silberg, 1987; Boring, Ottoboni, & Stark, 2016; MacNell, Driscoll, & Hunt, 2015; Rosen, 2017).

In a study of student course evaluations conducted by Kristina Martin of Texas Tech University and Jonathan Martin of Midland College, the researchers found that 15.6 percent of respondents referred to a female faculty member's personality, while similar comments were made by only 4.3 percent of the respondents when evaluating male professors. 32.7 percent of the male faculty members were referred to as "professor," while that title was used of only 15.6 percent of female faculty members. Conversely, 24.4 percent of women were referred to as "teacher" versus only 15.2 percent of the men (Mitchell & Martin, 2018).

A similar level of bias can be found in corporate employee appraisals (Bowen, Swim, & Jacobs 2000; Halpert, Wilson, & Hickman, 1993; Rivera & Tilcsik, 2019). The same qualities that are interpreted as demonstrating decisiveness and strong leadership potential in men are often dismissed as inflexibility and lack of collegiality in women. As one researcher has remarked,

> In one review I read, the manager noted, "Heidi seems to shrink when she's around others, and especially around clients, she needs to be more self-confident." But a similar problem—confidence in working with clients—was given a positive spin when a man was struggling with it: "Jim needs to develop his natural ability to work with people." (Cecchi-Dimeglio, 2017)

At this point, the objection might be raised that the discussion has gone rather far afield. It began by addressing the challenges encountered in the evaluation of administrators and governing boards but ended with issues that pertain to employee appraisals and the student course evaluations conducted for professors.

But the point is that these issues are all related. In addition to the problems specific to evaluating administrators and governing boards—the evaluators' frequent lack of familiarity with the organizational culture of higher education, overuse on self-evaluation, and the omission of tests for reliability and validity—the procedures often in place at colleges and universities have many of the same drawbacks found in *most* evaluation systems.

- There's no proof that they actually improve anyone's performance.
- Most evaluation systems are time consuming and anxiety provoking.
- They're probably influenced by such factors as the size and mission of the institution, the race, gender, and ethnicity of the per-

son(s) being evaluated, and recent history (such as the residual lack of trust left behind by a past CEO or board) at least as much as the actual performance of the administrator.
- The *halo effect* (i.e., the tendency for a reviewer's opinion about one aspect of someone's performance to influence his or her opinion about all other areas of performance) means that, despite all efforts to the contrary, most performance appraisals are little better than satisfaction surveys or popularity contests.

The questions that colleges and universities need to answer then are these: Could the procedure used to evaluate your CEO and governing board receive the approval as a valid research method by your school's own institutional review board (IRB)? And if not, why are you still using that procedure to make key decisions about some of your institution's most important stakeholders?

The fact is that many (perhaps most) colleges and universities either lack any coherent system for evaluating administrators and governing boards or engage in practices that are unlikely to produce meaningful results. The severity of this problem can be seen if we focus for a moment on just one component of most review processes: the instruments used to rate performance.

One common practice is for institutions to develop their own instruments and evaluation forms for evaluating governing boards and top administrators. There are certainly advantages for doing so. Locally developed instruments can be implemented at a far lower cost than purchasing professionally designed instruments and can be adapted more easily to reflect circumstances unique to that institution.

But this practice creates its own series of problems. In-house evaluation forms typically are written by people with little formal training and experience in appropriate research methods. As a result, the instruments used at many colleges or universities demonstrate some or all of the following problems.

- *Items are compound rather than focused.* For example, "The administrator is widely recognized as an effective leader and delegates responsibilities properly." Items like this example are referred to as *double-barreled questions*. They ask about more than one factor at once, in this case perceptions of effective leadership and proper delegation. Compound items confuse both the respondent ("How should I answer if I agree with only one of the two parts?") and the evaluator ("If the respondent answered *strongly agree*, to which part of the item is he or she strongly agreeing?").

- *Items are not actionable.* For example, "The board of trustees is the proper size." If the size of the board is set by the legislature or otherwise beyond the purview of the board to change, there's no reason to ask about it, and the question encourages participants not to participate in the process in the future. "Answering the same question over and over and not seeing anything change leads to participant frustration and a lack of interest in completing the evaluation form" (Phillips, 2007).

- *Items are ambiguous.* For example, "The administrator engages in an appropriate level of service." Items like this example are so vague that the results received are practically meaningless. The example does not specify whom the administrator is expected to serve: the institution's stakeholders? the community at large? his or her own academic discipline? Different respondents will interpret the question each in his or her own way, with the result that evaluators will not be able to determine clearly what advice to give the administrator.

- *Items don't include sufficient items.* For example, "How often should the board of regents meet in order to be as effective as possible? (a) Once a month, (b) Once a semester, (c) Once a year." Participants may believe that the best meeting schedule for the board is more frequently than once a month, less frequently than once a year, or on some other schedule not provided as an option. A question of this nature should be open-ended, such as, "In order for the board to be as effective as possible, I believe that the full board should meet _____ time(s) every _____ [you

may reply *day, week, month, semester, year*, or any other unit of time you regard as appropriate]."
- *Too many items are included.* It's not unusual for evaluation instruments to contain thirty or more items. This practice exacerbates the halo effect since a respondent's attention is likely to wander after the first few questions, and he or she will provide similar answers regardless of what the question is asking. Six items on an evaluation instrument is optimal, and in no cases should an instrument include more than twelve items. The consultancy firm Satrix Solutions recommends that evaluation forms be limited to issues that can be addressed within the next six months in order to keep them focused and to make it easier to track progress over time (see Beretta, 2014.)
- *Rating levels are inconsistent.* One of the most common types of question on evaluation forms a Likert Scale (pronounced LICK-ert, not LIE-kert), named for the social scientist Rensis Likert who, in 1932, invented a type of question that offered respondents a range of options that proceeded in gradual increments from one extreme to its opposite. But many Likert Scales are confusingly phrased or inconsistently spaced, such as "The board's work has been: [1] excellent, [2] superior, [3] good, [4] satisfactory, [5] unsatisfactory." On this scale, there are four gradations of acceptable work, but only one category for unacceptable work. The result is a leading question: The very structure of the scale biases the results since the respondent may feel encouraged to choose one of the four options for acceptable work. But there's also a problem with the consistency of the scale. It is peculiar. For example, is there really the same distance in performance between excellent and superior work as there is between good and satisfactory work? And what exactly is the difference between excellent work and superior work? Another problem that can occur is that, on the scale indicated, small numbers reflect better performance than large numbers. Many users will assume that large numbers are better than small numbers and, regardless of how

the scale is explained, answer according to what they assume is appropriate.
- *Items include implicit bias against women or other groups.* For example, Alice Eagley, the James Padilla Chair of Arts and Sciences and a professor of psychology at Northwestern University; Linda Carli, associate professor of psychology at Wellesley College; Herminia Ibarra, professor of organizational behavior at London Business School; and Otilia Obodaru, assistant professor of management at Rice University have found that women's leadership styles are undervalued in many evaluation processes. In the aggregate, women leaders tend to favor an open, consensus-building, and team-focused style of leadership rather than a strongly hierarchical, rank-based style. If an evaluation item asks respondents questions like, "Does the administrator appropriately follow the chain of command?" women were likely to be scored lower than men even though their own leadership was equally effective. (See Eagly & Carli, 2007 and Ibarra & Obodaru, 2009.)
- *Forms are not secure.* The goal in collecting perspectives from various stakeholder groups is to enable each participant to respond once and one time only. When dissemination of paper forms is not controlled through use of coded registration numbers and when online forms are not connected to individual respondents through two-step verification processes, it may be possible for people to submit multiple evaluations, skewing the results.

That's a long—some might even say damning—list of problems that are commonly found with in-house evaluation processes. And keep in mind that these are only the problems found in evaluation *forms*.

Forms themselves take no account of equally severe limitations that might be encountered in other aspects of the evaluation process: *who* provides the evaluator with information, *how* those results are interpreted, *which* judgments are made on the basis of those interpretations, *how* those judgments are conveyed to the person or group being evaluated, and so on.

So, other than avoiding the problems just outlined, can there be any strategy for evaluating administrators and governing boards fairly, accurately, and efficiently?

IMPROVING THE PROCESS OF BOARD AND ADMINISTRATOR EVALUATION

Fortunately, there's a long history of how employee evaluations should be done in the corporate world and how faculty evaluations should be done in the academic world that can be used to improve the process of board and administrator evaluation. For example, when Adobe's research indicated that neither supervisors nor employees found traditional performance reviews to be useful, they also developed an approach that served everyone's needs better.

Adobe calls its improved system the *Check In Process* and bases this process on the following principles:

- The person being reviewed meets regularly with his or her supervisor to discuss and adjust priorities. So, instead of being an annual process, Check In occurs on a schedule that makes sense for each person's unique situation.
- Check In conversations must occur at least quarterly, with more frequent feedback being the norm.
- The supervisor provides ongoing feedback and engages in constructive dialogue about how performance can be improved without providing any formal written review or maintaining documentation about what was said.
- The person who is reviewed isn't given a formal rating or ranking. The process is primarily qualitative not quantitative, formative not summative.
- The supervisor determines the employee's salary and makes appropriate equity adjustments annually based on the person's performance.

- Professionals in the office of human resources provide training to both supervisors and employees about how the Check In Process works, thus allowing both parties to have more constructive conversations.
- A centralized employee resource center provides assistance and answers questions whenever needed.[1]

Similar conclusions about how evaluations should be conducted have been reached by David Hassell, the CEO of 15Five, a company that assists businesses with continuous performance management.

> "The concept of manager as boss is antiquated," Hassell says emphatically. Today's leaders need to be coaches. The startup CEO goes on to explain that today's leaders need to understand each person's skill and morale levels, and goals. The leader's role today is to unlock people's potential. It's not to control people. Leaders are stewards. They have no control over people. Instead stewards have responsibility to care for those whom they lead. (Murphy, 2016)

As a result, 15Five recommends that annual performance reviews be replaced by the following process:

- Weekly check-ins in which employees take fifteen minutes to answer questions about their goals and activities, supervisors take five minutes to read and respond to these statements, and both reports can be reviewed by as many upper levels of the organizational hierarchy as are appropriate.
- These weekly check-ins also include brief questions about morale so that supervisors are constantly aware of the employee's level of satisfaction and engagement.
- Alignment occurs between the organization's top three priorities and the employee's immediate goals.
- One-on-one meetings are structured so as to coach employees through their most pressing challenges.
- A system of praise and reinforcement known as High Fives provides ongoing encouragement and, as 15Five says, makes "every

day Employee Appreciation Day!" (Employee Appreciation Software, 2019).
- The 360-degree evaluation is intended to be formative, not summative, thus avoiding people's fear that they're being constantly graded and found wanting.
- Formal performance conversations are held once each quarter, thus allowing those being reviewed sufficient time to reflect on their performance throughout the quarter and to identify ways of improving. These performance conversations are completely decoupled from compensation conversations so that everyone is clear about what is formative advice and what is summative appraisal.
- Finally, leaders connect employees to a shared purpose to illuminate why their work matters.[2]

Similar insights can be gained from other systems that have sought to minimize the effect that gender, ethnicity, and other factors unrelated to performance too often have on the evaluation process. In one of the studies on gender bias in performance evaluation that was mentioned earlier, Paola Cecchi-Dimeglio found that three strategies helped to reduce the impact of extraneous factors on the results of an appraisal.

> By using more-objective criteria, involving a broader group of reviewers, and adjusting the frequency of reviews, it is possible to remove subjective biases that creep in. Specifically, my field experiments at professional services firms suggest that the use of tailor-made, automated, real-time communication tools with instant feedback on employees' weekly performance from supervisors, colleagues, and clients can have dramatic results for women. As opposed to the traditional annual feedback system, these instruments were designed to remove bias from answers (e.g., the language of feedback options is gender-neutral) and help the reviewers to provide constructive feedback. The order of requested feedback was given careful consideration in the instruments' design, all in an effort to create a level playing field. (Cecchi-Dimeglio, 2017)

So, one critical step institutions can take in improving their evaluation processes is to have trained representatives from its IRB review the criteria used in evaluations to make certain they meet standards for objectivity and are phrased in such a way as to reduce the likelihood of bias, discontinue the practice of basing evaluations solely on observations made by the supervisory level (or, in the case of the governing board, self-evaluation), and phase out the traditional annual review in favor of a more frequent review schedule like the one recommended by 15Five.

Paola Cecchi-Dimeglio has a specific recommendation for how institutions can avoid the problem of basing evaluations only on self-evaluation or the observations of supervisors: "Invest in systems that crowdsource and continually collect data about the performance of people and teams. Crowdsourcing performance data throughout the year yields even better insights . . ." (Cecchi-Dimeglio, 2017).

Crowdsourcing, the practice of obtaining information from a large number of people usually via technology, can be an even more effective mechanism for continuous improvement than 360-degree assessment processes conducted once a year or less. (See, for example, Mosley [2012 and 2013], but also note the cautions raised by Fisher [2013].)

As Eric Mosely, the CEO of the performance management company Workhuman notes,

> By capturing input from many, rather than a few or just one, we're able to extend performance evaluations beyond a single point of failure to reveal how employees are truly performing and influencing others in the organization. (Mosley, 2012)

In addition to Workhuman, providers of crowdsourcing solutions include Grapevine Evaluations, Qmarkets, Brightidea, and Axero Solutions.

Colleges and universities can also improve their processes by making sure that the methods of data analysis and interpretation they require of their own professors in their research are applied to these evaluation processes. As this author has argued elsewhere, data about administrators is too frequently collected and analyzed in a manner that we'd never find acceptable in our own academic research. For example, we sometimes generalize from a very small sample size. It may sound informative to tell [an administrator or board], "100 percent of those who responded to the survey we distributed think that we need new leadership. . . ." But if that conclusion is based on only two people who completed the survey out of a pool larger than a hundred, the statement (although still technically accurate) is utterly meaningless. In addition, if we simply use averages with a relatively small sample size, our results may similarly be distorted. Saying something like, "Your score at serving as an effective advocate for your area averages 4.2 on a five-point scale" means something quite different if four people gave the person a perfect score of 5, with one disgruntled person giving a score of 1 (on this and every other question) than if that average results from a sample size of 239 respondents, all of whom considered each question carefully. (Buller, 2015, p. 383)

One way of improving this process is to complement the type of quantitative evaluation that is found in many systems of administrator and board review with a system of qualitative evaluation that makes it easier to track improvement over time and to examine areas of performance that are difficult to reduce to a Likert Scale. Peter Seldin and Mary Lou Higgerson (2002, pp. 6–7) have summarized some of the advantages that using portfolios has over reliance on numerical data alone:

- "Portfolios capture the individuality and complexity of academic administration" by being "grounded in the specifics and contexts of a particular administrative position in a particular college or university at a particular point in time" (Seldin & Higgerson, 2002, p. 6).
- Portfolios are a cooperative process in which the administrator or board choose items to be included, comment on them, and make their case. Systems of evaluation that are solely data-based often feel as though they are "imposed upon" the person or group being evaluated by an outside entity, particularly when the rubric or

instrument is not made public well in advance of the review process.
- Portfolios encourage boards and administrators to become more reflective about their performance. Rather than simply resulting in a score or series of scores that tell the boards or administrators *how well* they did, portfolios help boards and administrators consider *why* they did well and *how* they can do even better.
- "Portfolios can foster a culture of administrative professionalism" by being "prepared in consultation with others" and resulting in "a more public view of academic administration" (Seldin & Higgerson, 2002, p. 6).

Possible items that may be included in an administrative portfolio include the following:

- A statement of current responsibilities since what one CEO or governing board does is not necessarily identical to what others do. That statement can be annotated to indicate why those particular duties are appropriate priorities for the institution at this time.
- "A reflective statement by the administrator [or board] describing personal administrative philosophy, strategies and objectives, methodologies" (Seldin & Higgerson, 2002, p. 16).
- An analysis of the most important action taken by the board or administrator during the review period accompanied by a statement about why that action was important.
- An analysis of the most difficult decision made by the board or administrator during the review period accompanied by a statement about why that decision was difficult.
- Analysis of progress made on goals established during the previous evaluation.
- A list of goals to be accomplished during the period until the next evaluation.
- "Evidence of needs assessment of students, faculty, or other administrators" (Seldin & Higgerson, 2002, p. 16).

- Letters of external review by boards or CEOs at peer institutions.
- Letters of internal review by the CEO and vice presidents (for boards) or the board and vice presidents (for the CEO).
- A summary of the actions taken to improve administrative performance and efficiency since the last review.
- Explanations of any items in the portfolio that might appear unclear, contradictory, or misleading. (For other suggestions, see Seldin & Higgerson, 2002, pp. 16–20.)

Portfolio assessment thus makes the evaluation process both reflective (what was done and why) and forward looking (what *will* be done and why). It helps administrators and boards become more intentional about their leadership and less likely merely to react to situations as they occur.

WAYS OF IMPROVING EVALUATION INSTRUMENTS

The goal in adding portfolio assessments to the evaluation process isn't to *replace* the useful data gathered from evaluation instruments but to provide the improvement often needed for instruments used in evaluating upper administrators and governing boards.

Due to all the problems that arise from in-house instruments, most colleges and universities are probably better off partnering with a firm that specializes in conducting employee and supervisor evaluations than developing their own forms. These firms have expertise in developing instruments that produce reliable, valid, and statistically significant results and often have nationally or internationally normed data that can help institutions interpret scores within a larger context.

The challenge when selecting an outside vendor for board and administrative evaluations is, however, that each institution's goals and circumstances are distinctive. A standardized evaluation instrument can't capture all the nuances that make a college or university unique. For this reason, it's important to choose a provider that can tailor its evaluation instrument to capture the institution's specific needs but, at the same time, construct questions in such a way as to avoid the problems commonly found on in-house evaluation forms.

In addition to 15Five, which was mentioned earlier, vendors of customizable employee instruments include Culture Amp, Grapevine, AssessTEAM, and IDEA, the last of which is designed for the specific needs of higher education. New suppliers of employee and administrator evaluation forms appear all the time (and existing suppliers go out of business), so if you're interested in securing the services of an outside vendor for board or administrator evaluations, be sure to ask the companies that you're considering the following questions:

- What experience do you have working with colleges and universities?
- Is your system focused only on employee appraisal or can it be adapted for supervisor/manager appraisal as well?
- How customizable is your system?
- Will you work with us to develop a system that is reliable, valid, and statistically significant while still reflecting the unique nature and goals of our institution?
- Do you have a database of nationally or internationally normed results so that we can compare our results with others?

If your institution *does* choose to develop its own instrument, remember to follow all the guidelines mentioned earlier. It should be reviewed by your IRB or by trusted representatives from the IRB to make sure that it adheres to appropriate data-gathering procedures. It should, whenever possible, contain twelve or fewer items to be rated. Its items should be screened and then double-checked for implicit bias against women or other groups. Items should be properly focused, unambiguous, and actionable.

In addition, your institution should adhere to the following practices when designing its instrument and interpreting the results.

- *Phrase all items from the perspective of the evaluator, not the institution or the person being evaluated.* Whoever completes the evaluation form views the administrator or board from his or her own perspective. That perspective may be quite different from how the administrator or board views the world. For example, if an item is phrased as, "The board was accessible to all stakeholders of the institution," it asks the respondent to comment on matters that he or she cannot possibly know. The perception of one stakeholder group may be far different from that of another. It's better to say, "I found the board to be accessible to me." (See Kirkpatrick, 2008.)

- *If asking respondents to reply using a rating scale, use an odd number of categories.* If your scale ranges from 1 (extremely poor) to 5 (extremely good), it's intuitively obvious that 3 represents the midpoint between these two extremes. But if the scale ranges from 1 (extremely poor) to 10 (extremely good), respondents can be confused. How do they rate average or middling performance? As a 5? a 6? Can they write in 5.5? The result is that the evaluators begin to think more about how the form is designed than about the performance of the board or administrator. As Ken Phillips, the creator and chief architect of the learning evaluation methodology, Predictive Learning Analytics, explains,

> Odd numbered scales also more readily allow for the possibility of obtaining a normal bell shaped curve distribution of responses across the scale because it has an actual mid-point. Even numbered scales, on the other hand, increase the possibility of obtaining a skewed distribution of responses above or below the actual mathematical mid-point . . . because participants aren't allowed to register a neutral response. (Phillips, 2007)

- *On a numerical scale, only use verbal definitions to define the two extremes; let respondents determine what the intervening points mean to them.* Earlier it was noted that some evaluation instruments instruct the respondent to use a Likert Scale that is confusing, inconsistently spaced, or transforming the item into a leading question. You can avoid that problem by only labeling the two ends (e.g., Poor

and Excellent or Strongly Disagree and Strongly Agree), while allowing respondents to use their own judgment about consistent gradations between those two extremes.
- *Adopt a single rating scale for the entire instrument.* Respondents can become confused if one item has a scale with the first item ranging from Unsatisfactory to Highly Satisfactory, the next item ranging from Strongly Disagree to Strongly Agree, a third item ranging from Very Often to Never, and so on. That confusion can become worse when good performance is sometimes associated with the left side of the scale and at other times with the right. Probably the best approach is to combine the evaluator's perspective discussed above with a single consistent scale and phrase each item as a statement about effective performance with the respondent asked to reply from Strongly Disagree to Strongly Agree for each item.
- *Place low numbers indicating poor performance to the left, high numbers indicating good performance to the right.* As was mentioned earlier, respondents tend to assume that large numbers are better than small numbers, and so the best performance should be associated with the highest number on the scale. They also expect the numbers to proceed from left to right rather than from right to left. As Phillips observes, constructing rating scales in the reverse order "runs counter to the way we count and can create problems when participants are in a hurry to complete the evaluation form and mistakenly mark their responses at the right end of the scale thinking these are the better responses" (Phillips, 2007). As a result, forms are less confusing when the left extreme of the scale is labeled something like 1 = Strongly Disagree, with the right extreme of the scale labeled something like 5 = Strongly Agree.
- *When calculating average scores, use modes and medians not arithmetic means.* Most evaluation systems that use response forms require that those forms be aggregated in some way. The idea is to figure out how "most people" or "the typical person" feels about the performance of the board or administrator. The most common way of aggregating the results is to calculate the arithmetic mean: you

simply add the value assigned to each answer together and divide the result by the number of values you have. But arithmetic means are notoriously susceptible to outliers, particularly when the number of values is not large. And typically, there *aren't* a large number of values in board and administrator evaluations. If board members evaluate the president, there might be twenty or fewer responses to each question. If the president and vice presidents evaluate the board, the number of responses can be even lower. Institutions tend to calculate arithmetic means because most people are familiar with the concept. Some people even assume that the terms *average* and *arithmetic mean* are exact synonyms. But one vice president who has a grudge against the board can skew the results significantly. So can one board member who is an ardent supporter of the president when other board members are less satisfied with his or her performance.

- Other problems also exist with arithmetic means. Spreadsheets can calculate results to as many decimal places as one likes, resulting in "average" scores of 3.78 or even 2.3145. But while those results have the *appearance* of being precise, they actually aren't meaningful. With a Likert Scale, only whole numbers, usually 1 through 5, are possible responses. No one can rate the president or the board 1.46375. And the rule of thumb of tabulating results is that *your result can only be as precise as your least precise bit of input data*. As a result, aggregated scores on evaluations should always be reported as whole numbers, not as decimals. The best way to accomplish this goal is to calculate the *median* (the midpoint in a series of values when they're ordered from smallest to largest) and the *mode* (the most common value in a set of numbers). The median will tell you what "the typical person" feels about the performance of the board or administrator, and the mode will tell you what "most people" feel. And remember, that's what you were looking for in the first place.
- *Be very skeptical of single composite scores.* Some review processes involve calculation of an average score for each item on the survey instrument and a single composite score for all items, "grading" the board or president with a 4.8, a 3.75, or another such number, but

these scores are almost always meaningless. In the worst-case scenario, the composite score is simply an "average of the averages" for each item, but only two people may have answered three of the questions, while twenty-four people answers three other questions. "Averaging the averages" privileges the responses of two people to the detriment of twenty-four people because it assumes that a pair of voices has the same significance as two dozen voices. Even in the best-case scenario, where all individual responses to all questions are averaged, the result is problematic. It assumes that each question is equally important, but one question may reflect the core responsibilities of the president or board while another question may reflect only preferences or value-added components. Unless the responses to each question are weighted for their significance, composite scores generally tell you very little.

- *Include open-ended questions, but not too many.* Those who process evaluation forms like questions with Likert Scales because the responses can easily be aggregated and because a numerical score gives the impression of mathematical precision. But these forms also frequently include open-ended questions since respondents may wish to provide a more complete context for their answers or offer information they weren't asked about. It's useful to provide one or two open-ended questions such as, "Please use the space below if you would like to explain or provide more complete content for one or more of your answers" and, "Is there anything we should know that we didn't ask you about? If so, provide that information in the space below." But too many open-ended questions make it difficult for reviewers to process information and obtain a clear overall picture of the board or CEO's performance. In addition, some evaluators will be deterred from completing evaluation forms with too many open-ended questions because answering such questions is time consuming. The result is that certain voices important to the evaluation process end up not being heard.

CONCLUSION

Evaluation of high-ranking administrators and governing boards can be valuable to schools and help them function more effectively. Even beyond their utility, however, these evaluations are important because increasingly legislatures, governors, and accrediting agencies are requiring them. But too many colleges and universities follow evaluation practices that are flawed and inefficient, leaving those institutions vulnerable to complaints and possibly even lawsuits.

Higher education needs to do better. Both research and years of experience by HR professionals and systems of faculty evaluation have resulted in an understanding of what works and what doesn't work in the area of performance appraisal. The general principles outlined in this chapter can improve the evaluation process.

But in order to create truly effective evaluation processes for administrators and governing boards, it's necessary to examine the differences between how CEOs need to be evaluated and how governing boards (and/or their individual members) need to be evaluated. Those are the topics that will be explored in the pages that follow.

KEY POINTS IN THIS CHAPTER

- State legislatures and regional accrediting bodies are increasingly mandating evaluation of high-ranking administrators and governing boards.
- Some institutions don't know where to begin when developing a comprehensive evaluation process. Other institutions have a process in place that doesn't meet high enough standards for how information should be collected and interpreted.
- Using self-evaluations alone has been demonstrated to be an unreliable and ineffective means of evaluation.
- Relying on single-point-of-view evaluation systems (such as appraisal only by one's direct supervisor) results in a limited and, in many cases, a biased view of the administrator or board's performance.

- There is a substantial body of research indicating that traditional ways of conducting performance evaluations are severely flawed and recommending specific improvements.
- There is also a substantial body of research indicating that the faculty evaluation system used by many colleges and universities is biased. Since it is not uncommon to base the procedures used for evaluating boards and administrators on these faculty evaluation systems, the result can be a process that does not adequately reflect the true performance of the board or administrator.
- In-house evaluation forms are particularly problematic. It is far preferable for institutions to work with an experienced outside vendor to develop a custom-made evaluation form that is statistically valid and follows industry best practices.
- A large number of in-house forms developed for evaluating boards and administrators contain too many items, poorly phrased questions, ambiguous and inconsistent scales, and numerous other defects that limit their usefulness.
- Annual evaluations are less likely to improve performance than more frequent, less formal discussions about the progress of the administrator or the board.
- Crowdsourcing and portfolio evaluation are valuable tools that are infrequently used as part of the evaluation process.

REFERENCES

Accreditation Standards: Accrediting Commission for Community and Junior Colleges of the Western Association of Schools and Colleges. 2012. https://accjc.org/wp-content/uploads/Accreditation-Standards-for-Reviews-through-Fall-2015.pdf.

Arubayi, E. A., & Delta State University (Delta State, Nigeria). 2003. *Improvement of instruction and teacher effectiveness in tertiary institutions: are students' ratings reliable and valid?* Abraka, Nigeria: Delta State University.

Basow, S. A., & Silberg, N. L. 1987. Student evaluations of college professors: Are female and male professors rated differently? *Journal of Educational Psychology*, 79(3): 308–14.

Beretta, J. 2014. Top ten common problems in designing effective survey questions. https://www.satrixsolutions.com/blog/top-ten-common-problems-designing-effective-survey-questions/.

Boring, A., K. Ottoboni, & Stark, P. B. 2016. Student evaluations of teaching (mostly) do not measure teaching effectiveness, *ScienceOpen Research* 1–11.

Bowen, C.-C., J. K. Swim, & R. R. Jacobs. 2000. Evaluating gender biases on actual job performance of real people: A meta-analysis. *Journal of Applied Social Psychology, 30*(10): 2194–215.

Buller, J. L., & Reeves, D. M. 2018. *The five cultures of academic development: Crossing boundaries in higher education fundraising.* Washington, DC: CASE.

Cecchi-Dimeglio, P. 2017. How gender bias corrupts performance reviews, and what to do about it. *Harvard Business Review.* https://hbr.org/2017/04/how-gender-bias-corrupts-performance-reviews-and-what-to-do-about-it.

Culbertson, S. S., Henning, J. B., & Payne, S. C. 2013. Performance appraisal satisfaction: The role of feedback and goal orientation. *Journal of Personnel Psychology, 12*(4): 189–95.

d'Apollonia, S., & Abrami, P. C. 1997. Navigating student ratings of instruction. *American Psychologist, 52*(11): 1198–1208.

Dunning, D., Heath, C., & Suls, J. M. 2004. Flawed self-assessment: Implications for health, education, and the workplace. *Psychological Science in the Public Interest, 5*(3): 69–106.

Eagly, A. H., & Carli, L. L. 2007. Women and the labyrinth of leadership. *Harvard Business Review, 85*(9): 63–71.

Eiszler, C. F. 2002. College students' evaluations of teaching and grade inflation. *Research in Higher Education, 43*(4): 483–501.

Employee Appreciation Software: 15Five. 2019. https://www.15five.com/high-fives/.

Fisher, A. 2013. Should performance reviews be crowdsourced? *Fortune.* https://fortune.com/2013/10/08/should-performance-reviews-be-crowdsourced/.

Germain, M.-L., & Scandura, T. A. 2005. Grade inflation and student individual differences as systematic bias in faculty evaluations. *Journal of Instructional Psychology, 32*(1): 58–67.

Gravestock, P., & Gregor-Greenleaf, E. 2008. *Student course evaluations: Research, models and trends.* Toronto, Canada: Higher Education Quality Council of Ontario.

Griffin, B. W. 2004. Grading leniency, grade discrepancy, and student ratings of instruction. *Contemporary Educational Psychology, 29*(4): 410–25.

Halpert, J. A., Wilson, M. L., & Hickman, J. L. 1993. Pregnancy as a source of bias in performance appraisals. *Journal of Organizational Behavior, 14*(7): 649–63.

Ibarra, H., and O. Obodaru. 2009. Women and the vision thing. *Harvard Business Review, 87*(1): 62–70.

Kirkpatrick, J. 2008. The new world level 1 reaction sheets. https://www.kirkpatrickpartners.com/Portals/0/Storage/The%20new%20world%20level%201%20reaction%20sheets.pdf.

Kluger, A. N., & DeNisi, A. 1996. The effects of feedback interventions on performance: A historical review, a meta-analysis, and a preliminary feedback intervention theory. *Psychological Bulletin, 119* (2), 254–84.

MacNell, L., Driscoll, A., & Hunt, A. N. 2015. What's in a name: Exposing gender bias in student ratings of teaching. *Innovative Higher Education, 40*(4): 291–303.

Marsh, H. W., & Roche, L. A. 2000. Effects of grading leniency and low workload on students' evaluations of teaching: Popular myth, bias, validity, or innocent bystanders? *Journal of Educational Psychology, 92*(1), 202–28.

Mitchell, K. M. W., & Martin, J. 2018. Gender bias in student evaluations. *Ps: Political Science & Politics, 51*(3): 648–52.

Mosley, E. 2012. Crowdsource your performance reviews. *Harvard Business Review.*https://hbr.org/2012/06/crowdsource-your-performance-r.

Mosley, E. 2013. *The crowdsourced performance review: How to use the power of social recognition to transform employee performance.* New York, NY: McGraw-Hill.

Murphy, S. 2016. The annual performance review is insulting, ineffective, and outdated. Let it die. https://slate.com/business/2016/01/kill-the-annual-performance-review.html.

NWCCU Standards. 2019. https://www.nwccu.org/accreditation/standards-policies/standards/.

Phillips, K. 2007. *Eight tips on developing valid Level 1 evaluation forms.* https://tdpiedmont.org/Resources/Documents/8%20Tips%20On%20Developing%20Valid%20Level1%20Evaluation%20Forms.pdf.

Principles of Accreditation: Southern Association of Colleges and Schools Commission on Colleges. 2018. http://www.sacscoc.org/pdf/2018PrinciplesOfAcreditation.pdf.

Resource Manual for the Principles of Accreditation. 2018. http://www.sacscoc.org/pdf/2018%20POA%20Resource%20Manual.pdf.

Rivera, L. A., & Tilcsik, A. 2019. Scaling down inequality: Rating scales, gender bias, and the architecture of evaluation. *American Sociological Review, 84*(2): 248–74.

Rodriguez, C. 2017. Performance review peril: Adobe study shows office workers waste time and tears. https://news.adobe.com/press-release/corporate/performance-review-peril-adobe-study-shows-office-workers-waste-time-and.

Rosen, A. S. 2017. Correlations, trends, and potential biases among publicly accessible web-based student evaluations of teaching. *Assessment & Evaluation in Higher Education, 1,* 1–14.

Seldin, P., & Higgerson, M. L. 2002. *The administrative portfolio: A practical guide to improved administrative performance and personnel decisions.* Bolton, MA: Anker.

Standards for Accreditation: New England Commission of Higher Education. 2016. https://www.neche.org/resources/standards-for-accreditation/.

Standards for Accreditation and Requirements of Affiliation: Middle States Commission on Higher Education. 2019. https://www.msche.org/standards/.

Tugend, A. 2019. To improve leadership, some colleges take a cue from industry: 360-degree reviews. *The Chronicle of Higher Education.* https://www.chronicle.com/article/To-Improve-Leadership-Some/246116.

Unlock the Potential of Your Entire Workforce: 15Five. 2019. https://www.15five.com/?_bt=350206624300&_bk=%2B15five&_bm=b&_bn=g&_bg=72572959327&gclid=Cj0KCQjwsvrpBRCsARIsAKBR_0IPkKRt2HCYCAi1SAiYp3O0XrQ_K3occZ46loT_F6p0rZ-sSl7HcZIaAuHsEALw_wcB.

RESOURCES

Buller, J. L. 2012. *Best practices in faculty evaluation: A practical guide for academic leaders.* San Francisco, CA: Jossey-Bass.

Coens, T., & Jenkins, M. 2002. *Abolishing performance appraisals: Why they backfire and what to do instead.* San Francisco, CA: Berrett-Koehler.

Dipboye, R. L. January 1, 1985. Some neglected variables in research on discrimination in appraisals. *Academy of Management Review, 10*(1): 116–27.

Farmer, C. H. 1978. The faculty role in administrator evaluation. *New Directions for Higher Education, 22,* 41–50.

Flynn, P. M., Haynes, K., & Kilgour, M. A. 2017. *Overcoming challenges to gender equality in the workplace: Leadership and innovation.* New York, NY: Routledge.

Seldin, P. 1988. *Evaluating and developing administrative performance: A practical guide for academic leaders*. San Francisco, CA: Jossey-Bass.

Slesinger, L. H. 1996. *Self-assessment for nonprofit governing boards*. Washington, DC: National Center for Nonprofit Boards.

NOTES

1. See www.adobe.com/check-in.html. The bullet points are a paraphrase, not a quote.

2. See Unlock the Potential of Your Entire Workforce (2019) and Murphy (2016). These bullet points are a paraphrase, not a quote.

2

HOW TO EVALUATE ADMINISTRATORS EFFECTIVELY

What are the best ways to evaluate presidents, chancellors, and other high-ranking administrators at colleges and universities? In order to answer this question methodically, it's important to back up several steps and ask a number of far more global questions: What does it mean to evaluate someone? Why do institutions of higher education conduct evaluations? What purposes are these evaluations supposed to serve?

These questions need to be asked because many people involved in the evaluation process either have no idea what they hope to achieve through administrative evaluations or believe that they know why these evaluations are performed even though the purposes they have in mind may not agree at all with how others at their school would describe the process. As was seen in chapter 1, they may be evaluating administrators simply because those evaluations are required but not because they're aware of all the benefits that could result from this process.

To start at the beginning, therefore, it's helpful to understand that personnel evaluations are conducted to determine the following:

- how well someone is performing,
- how his or her performance could be improved,
- whether the person qualifies for some sort of meritorious recognition,

- whether the person is performing poorly enough that he or she should be given a mandatory performance improvement plan, reassigned, or terminated,
- what progress has been made on the person's current goals,
- what the person's future goals should be, and
- how the person's goals and the institution's goals can be better aligned.

Of these objectives, it's likely that most people would say that the most important is determining how well the person being evaluated is performing.

But what does the phrase "determining how well someone is performing" actually mean? At its most basic level, institutions accomplish this task in performance appraisals by assessing how well the person is performing his or her fundamental duties (as defined in the *job description*), achieving overarching goals (as defined by his or her *strategic objectives*), and using effective approaches to perform those duties and achieve those goals (i.e., engaging in effective *tactics and practices*).

For this reason, a college or university can't expect its process for evaluating senior administrators to be effective if it does not regularly ask itself three sets of questions.

1. *Job description.* Do the job descriptions of our senior administrators adequately reflect what those administrators should be doing in order to fulfill our school's mission and vision? Do the job descriptions of our senior administrators adequately reflect what we actually expect those administrators to do?
2. *Strategic objectives.* What should our institution be doing in the next five to ten years that it is not doing now? What should it be doing in the next five to ten years even better than it is doing now? Do the administrator's long-term plans reflect those strategic objectives?
3. *Tactics and practices.* What style of leadership and management would be best suited to the duties outlined in the administrator's job description? What style of leadership and management would

be best suited to achieve the strategic objectives that have been outlined? How might an administrator's style of leadership and management need to be adapted in the face of different challenges, opportunities, and changing circumstances?

Because the environment in which colleges and universities operate changes so quickly, consideration of these questions will need to recur every two or three years.

PROBLEMS WITH JOB DESCRIPTIONS

Making it a priority to update the job descriptions of CEOs, vice presidents, and deans is particularly important because what these administrators do evolves over time. Moreover, good administrators effectively create their own "job descriptions" by stretching themselves and the units they supervise in ways that could not have been anticipated when they were originally appointed to their positions.

There are also other problems with administrative job descriptions at many colleges and universities. Too frequently, the job description of the president or chancellor is written by the governing board and, as a result, focuses heavily on the CEO's relationship with the board, not with the full range of his or her stakeholders.

For example, of the twelve responsibilities that the policies of the University of New Mexico assigns to its president, four mention the duties the president has to the board, only one mentions students (two if a reference to "intercollegiate athletics" is also included), and none mention the faculty, except a generic reference to "administration of the personnel system" (University of New Mexico, 2016).

But these board-focused job descriptions aren't only found at flagship universities. The policies of St. Charles Community College in Cottleville, Missouri, also lists twelve specific responsibilities in the president's job description, *more than half* of which concern the CEO's duties to the board. In fact, one of those responsibilities—"Perform such other duties as may be assigned or delegated by the Board of

Trustees"—is so broad that its reach is almost limitless (St. Charles Community College, 2019).

The problem with CEO job descriptions that deal so extensively with how presidents and chancellors interact with the board is that they frequently result in evaluation systems that de-emphasize or even ignore the responsibilities senior administrators have with other internal and external stakeholders. That situation is exacerbated when *the only group that evaluates the president or chancellor is the board itself*.

Furthermore, while written job descriptions of senior officers can be quite similar at many institutions, what administrators actually do can vary considerably from one school to another. The president of a large research university faces very different expectations from the president of a small church-affiliated college or a two-year community college with open enrollment. And that situation becomes even more dramatic at other levels of the senior administration.

What constitutes success for a provost is very different from what constitutes success for the vice president for student affairs or the vice president for business affairs. The daily duties of a dean vary widely depending on whether the dean is in charge of the medical school, the college of liberal arts, the honors college, the graduate program, or the library. Those duties can even change from year to year within the same unit. Nevertheless, some institutions use exactly the same appraisal process and evaluation form for all their vice presidents and all their deans.

As a result, this chapter will guide institutions in how to define what success actually looks like for each administrative position and how to set comparably high standards even though the factors that are measured will vary considerably from one administrator to another and for the same administrator from year to year.

It's clear, therefore, that if colleges and universities are going to have meaningful evaluations of the senior leadership teams, they're going to have to follow the recommendations presented in chapter 1, regularly update the job descriptions for the person being evaluated, avoid processes that appraise performance based only on the supervisor's perspective, assess progress toward strategic objectives, and measure the effectiveness of the administrator's tactics and practices.

LEARNING FROM THE FACULTY EVALUATION PROCESS

Fortunately, accomplishing these goals doesn't mean that the process used to evaluate administrators has to be developed from scratch. There's already a substantial body of research and experience relating to what works and what doesn't work in evaluating faculty members, and many of these insights can be carried over into administrative evaluations.

For example, in chapter 1, it was suggested that portfolio evaluation can provide a much more nuanced view of someone's performance than that which results from numbers on a rating sheet alone. That research on administrative portfolios, performed by Peter Seldin and others, originated in work first done with faculty members, beginning with *teaching portfolios* and later expanding into *academic portfolios*. (See Seldin, Miller, & Seldin, 2010; Seldin & Miller, 2009.)

Other work, done by Raoul Arreola of the University of Tennessee Health Science Center, provides additional insights into how faculty evaluations may be more consistent and thus how administrative evaluations might be improved. When performing faculty evaluations, Arreola recommends a process that can be described in terms of five sequential steps.

1. *Identify the factors that will be evaluated:* What makes a college professor good at what he or she does? What observable or measurable behaviors are associated with that good performance?
2. *Identify the sources of information to be used in the evaluation:* How can the person or group conducting the evaluation observe and measure the behaviors it has identified as significant?
3. *Weigh the factors and their associated behaviors by priority:* How important is each component of good performance? How

important is each observable/measurable behavior as a source of information?
4. *Weigh the sources of information by their reliability and significance:* Are certain sources of information more important or reliable than others? If so, how much value should be assigned to each source?
5. *Create a formula to calculate the result.*

For example, it's not uncommon for colleges and universities to say that the factors that constitute being a good college professor are teaching, research, and service. Arreola says that observation alone isn't enough.

One also has to ask how one *recognizes* effectiveness in teaching, research, and service. Then one has to weigh those factors in terms of their priority. In evaluating teaching effectiveness, is a student's success in subsequent classes more or less important than the percentage of students who assign the professor high ratings on course evaluations? In evaluating research effectiveness, are the number of refereed publications more or less important than the amount of external funding the professor brings in?

Next, one has to consider the reliability and significance of different sources of information. After all, students, faculty colleagues, and the professor's supervisor can all tell you something about the logical flow of a professor's course design. But are all those sources of information equally important and trustworthy? If not, how much weight should be assigned to the information received from each source?

Since the final step in the process is a formula based on weighted scores, Arreola's system of faculty evaluation results in a single numerical result for each faculty member that's tailored to the specific duties that the professor has but that also can be easily compared to the results of other faculty members.

On a 5-point scale, a professor who scores a 4.72 is regarded as having performed better than a professor who scores a 3.51, even though each professor may have different responsibilities. For a research professor, research is simply given more weight. For a teaching professor, instruction is given more weight. Similar consideration can be given to classroom teaching versus online teaching, graduate versus undergraduate courses, and so on.

The weakness of this system is that it lapses into the fallacy of mathematical precision. It's hard to argue that a score of 4.83 is truly better than a score of 4.82 in terms of statistical significance. And while the scores result from behaviors that are "measured," the vast majority of these measurements result from subjective impressions on Likert Scales. So, 4.12 may *look* a lot more specific than "most people agree with this statement," but for all practical purposes, those two outcomes are identical.

Nevertheless, the lessons to be learned from Arreola's system involve the process that is used. This approach forces one to ask important questions such as, "Where are we getting our information?" and, "How significant is this piece of information relative to others?" If one were, therefore, to adapt Arreola's system to administrative evaluation, avoid the problems resulting from the fallacy of mathematical precision, and incorporate the other recommendations presented earlier in this book, what would the resulting system look like?

DEVELOPING A NEW APPROACH TO ADMINISTRATIVE EVALUATIONS

By adapting the lessons of how data is properly collected and by drawing on the experience gained from years of faculty evaluation and personnel appraisals in the corporate world, it's possible to develop a fifteen-step approach to administrative evaluation that is far more effective than what most colleges and universities do now.

Step One

Identify the group that is most appropriate for supervising the evaluation process.

In order for administrative evaluations to be conducted effectively, it's necessary for *some* person or group to be in charge of the process.

But supervising the evaluation process isn't the same thing as supervising the administrator. In fact, in order to avoid having the results skewed by a single point of view, it's preferable that the administrator's supervisor *not* be the person in charge of the evaluation.

The best approach is to develop an administrative evaluation subcommittee that supervises the evaluation process of the president/chancellor, all vice presidents/chancellors, and all deans. This subcommittee should include representatives from the school's IRB who are trained in econometrics, psychometrics, or other statistical methods commonly used in the social sciences.

This *supervisory subcommittee* should also include the president/chancellor, one or more vice presidents/chancellors, and one or more deans who would recuse themselves from any aspect of the process in which they themselves would be evaluated. The remainder of the subcommittee should consist of representatives from whichever stakeholder groups (such as the faculty, staff, governing board, or external reviewers) that the institution regards as most appropriate for its traditions and missions. The subcommittee should be relatively small. A group of from eight to twelve people works best.

Since a well-trained subcommittee is the best option for supervising the administrative evaluation process, the person or group in charge of the evaluation will be referred to below as the subcommittee or supervisory subcommittee for the sake of consistency. If, for whatever reason, your institution decides to have the process supervised by an individual person or some other group, simply substitute the title of that person or group for the word *subcommittee* in the steps that follow.

Step Two

Have the supervisory subcommittee supervise the process of determining the most critical functions of each position being evaluated.

Since job descriptions don't provide full and complete descriptions of what administrators actually do, it's important for those supervising the review process to identify each administrator's real responsibilities, strategic objectives, day-to-day tactics, and leadership practices before attempting to conduct an evaluation. Is the institution currently in the midst of a capital campaign? Are there enrollment challenges that need to be overcome? Have morale issues led to the departure of members of the faculty and staff? Have those reporting to the administrator received appropriate guidance and support?

These issues may be addressed tangentially in the administrator's job description through phrases like, "the president is responsible for overseeing both human and financial resources in a manner that ensures accountability," but what do these statements actually mean in terms of what the president should be doing? Is the institution currently growing, sustaining its current size, retrenching, or something else?

If the president has been charged with "leading the institution in the acquisition of additional resources," does that mean working with the legislature to secure additional state support, encouraging researchers to apply for additional external grants, meeting with potential donors to secure unrestricted funds, reaching out to industry to develop sponsored research, or something else?

When asked the latter question, most governing boards will probably respond, "The president should be doing all of that," but these expectations aren't reasonable, and they aren't easy to evaluate. A better question to ask is this: "What precisely are the critical functions of *this* president at *this* institution at *this* time?" Being able to answer that question not only helps the president; it also helps the board clarify their own understanding of the institution's current needs.

At the level of vice presidents and deans, determining critical functions should take account of the reality that different vice presidents and deans do very different things. The goal of the subcommittee in consultation with other stakeholders, therefore, should be to determine the actual duties of this particular administrator at this particular time in the history of the institution. Trying to conduct a performance review without making this determination is likely to result in an evaluation that's neither fair nor meaningful.

Step Three

Describe specific behaviors or results that constitute success in each of the key functions that have been identified.

Even after the administrator's critical functions have been clarified, it's not yet possible to evaluate how well he or she performs those critical functions until success (or at least acceptable performance) in those areas has been clarified.

For example, if one of the president's most important responsibilities involves the acquisition of additional resources, what does success in acquiring additional funds look like? If the president raised one additional dollar, would that be enough? Would it take a million dollars? Ten million dollars? Or does the phrase "acquire additional resources" simply mean that the president is supposed to raise more money than last year? Without answers to these questions, the president won't know what his or her charge actually is, and the board won't know how to evaluate the president's performance in any meaningful way.

Critical functions are best phrased in such a way that they either involve an assignment that can be quantified ("Increase undergraduate student enrollment by at least a thousand students") or are easily validated as to whether or not a required action occurred ("Submit a completed reaccreditation application to the school's regional accreditor"). Fortunately, colleges and universities have a great deal of experience with how to phrase these expectations due to their work with outcomes assessment.

For example, one template commonly used in the assessment of learning outcomes has the following structure:

> By [specific point in the program], [all or an acceptable percentage of] students majoring in [program] will be able to [general action phrase] by [performing specific observable activity]. (Buller, 2012, p. 357)

This type of template results in measurable outcomes like the following:

> By the beginning of their second year, 90 percent of students majoring in the classics will be able to demonstrate proficiency in reading Latin by being able to translate at sight a three-hundred word passage of either Cicero or Seneca with no more than five errors as determined by the Sight Translation Committee. (Buller, 2012, p. 357)

Phrased in this way, the learning outcome makes it easy for the program to answer the question, "Did we meet our objective or not?"

For administrators, this sort of template, already familiar to most faculty members and academic leaders, could be modified to something like the following:

> By [specific point in time], the [title of administrator] will have demonstrated [general action phrase] by [achieving, completing, or reaching a specified numerical target in performing an observable activity].

Examples of critical functions produced by such a template would look like this:

> By the end of the academic year, the dean of the College of Engineering will have demonstrated a commitment to meeting international benchmarks by completing the university's application for accreditation by ABET (formerly known as the Accreditation Board for Engineering and Technology).
>
> By the time of the fifth-year review, the chancellor will have demonstrated significant improvement of the university's athletic program by achieving a ranking within the top ten of the division in no fewer than three intercollegiate sports.
>
> By the start of the next fiscal year, the vice president for business will have demonstrated fiscal responsibility by reducing the amount of deferred maintenance by at least 50 percent of its current level.

Phrasing an administrator's critical function in this way has three benefits. It alerts the administrator to his or her most important tasks for the future. It makes it easy for anyone to determine objectively whether the function has been performed by the date assigned. And it describes the function in a way that will be familiar to most of the people who work in higher education today.

Step Four

Rank the specific behaviors or results that constitute success in order of priority.

In most cases, after having identified the specific behaviors or results that constitute the administrator's successful performance, the subcommittee in charge of the process will end up with a rather long list of expectations. That's perfectly normal. In order to succeed as higher education administrators these days, people *need* to be able to perform at a level of advanced proficiency in many areas. But that doesn't mean that all the behaviors or results the subcommittee has identified are of equal importance.

The next step in the evaluation process should be, therefore, to rank the behaviors or results that have been identified in priority order. That task can seem overwhelming, particularly if the list that's been generated contains twenty or more items. So, the best approach isn't to try to rank all the items at once, but rather to look at only two items at a time.

Let's suppose a subcommittee has identified twenty-six behaviors or results that constitute successful performance by the institution's president or chancellor. One way of proceeding is to identify these items by assigning each of them a different letter of the English alphabet.

Then compare the first two items, A and B: Which of these two items seems more important than the other? Keep that item, set aside the other, and proceed to the next item on the list. Thus, if Item A was regarded as more important than Item B, the next comparison will be between Item A and Item C: Which of *these* two items now seems more important than the other?

Keep proceeding through the entire list in this fashion. At the end, you'll have identified the one item that is the highest priority in the president or chancellor's performance. Label it Task Number One and then do the same thing through the remaining twenty-five items to identify Task Number Two, Task Number Three, and so on. In a relatively small amount of time, you'll end up with the prioritized list of administrative functions that you were looking for. This process is called the *paired comparisons method of sorting*, and it's a great timesaver when you are developing or refining an evaluation process.

Step Five

Identify objective and reliable sources of information about those specific behaviors and results.

Once the essential tasks of the administrator have been ranked in order of their importance, you have to decide how you'll gather insights into the performance of those tasks. Obviously, you'll ask the administrators to perform a self-evaluation but, as was discussed in chapter 1, self-evaluations alone aren't enough. You'll learn how the administrator *perceives* his or her own performance, but people are often overly critical or overly complimentary when they evaluate their own performance.

Supervisors can provide you with one type of information. For example, boards can tell you how well the CEO is doing in terms of meeting their expectations, keeping them informed about critical issues, making progress on the strategic plan, and similar issues. CEOs can tell you how well the vice presidents are doing in terms of advocating effectively for their areas, providing suitable guidance to others in their divisions, being fiscally responsible, interacting appropriately with other vice presidents, and so on.

But those who report to the supervisors might have a completely different perspective, and their insights are valuable, too. What looks like strong leadership to a supervisor might appear to be inflexibility and high-handedness to subordinates. A supervisor doesn't always see how often administrators meet with those who report to them, how accessible they are, whether they're willing to collaborate, the degree to which they support decisions that have been delegated to them, and the like.

Peers, too, can provide you with valuable information. How well is the CEO regarded by presidents and chancellors of other institutions? Is he or she active in state or regional meetings? Is the CEO regarded as visionary or a leader among leaders? Similarly, other vice presidents can tell you whether a vice president is seen as a team player or someone who cares only about the interests of his or her own division.

As you go through your prioritized list of critical behaviors and results, make a note of how you'll collect the information you need about how well the administrator performed in those areas. Where you have more than one source of information about a task, indicate the relative degree of objectivity, reliability, and significance of each source.

For instance, you're likely to learn something about the administrator's leadership style from his or her own self-evaluation, as well as from the information provided by supervisors, peers, and subordinates. But are all of those sources equally important? If not, how would you weigh the different sources in terms of what you'll learn from them?

Step Six

Pare the specific behaviors or results that constitute success down to a reasonable number.

At this point in your evaluation process, you're still likely to have a rather long list of duties that the administrator should be performing. But collecting information about thirty or forty responsibilities will make your process unwieldy. In addition, the formative advice you give the administrator after the process won't be as helpful as it could be when your list of recommendations is so long that the truly important items get lost.

Since your list of desired behaviors and results is in priority order, focus on the most significant tasks. In chapter 1, we saw that it's best to include no more than six to twelve items on an evaluation instrument.

Use that same number as a rule of thumb for the number of responsibilities to include in your evaluation.

Doing so doesn't mean simply lopping off any item on your prioritized list that doesn't fit into the top six to twelve. Remember that different sources of information are more reliable than others in different areas. If you decide to focus on six responsibilities, the six items you include on the evaluation form you give the administrator's supervisor, peers, and subordinates need not be the same. Similarly, the items the administrator rates on his or her own self-evaluation form need not overlap entirely with the work products he or she includes in an administrative portfolio.

In this way, even if you ask each stakeholder group participating in the process to focus only a small number of activities, you'll still get a substantial body of information. Since there will be (and in fact should be) at least some degree of overlap in the questions posed to different groups, even asking six questions of each group will give you good, reliable information about at least ten of the highest priorities on your list of duties. That's a very manageable subset of responsibilities to focus on in an administrative evaluation process.

Step Seven

Communicate these criteria to the administrator at the start of the evaluation period.

The criteria that the subcommittee has established are something like a grading rubric, a concept that is familiar to nearly everyone who has a background in education. On a standard grading rubric, standards are defined in various areas of achievement, and levels of performance are assigned within that standard.

For example, excellent performance in spelling, punctuation, and grammar may be defined as two or fewer errors per ten pages of writing, good performance as three or four errors per ten pages, satisfactory performance as five or six errors, and unsatisfactory performance as seven or more errors. Similar levels of performance might be specified for such areas as use of supporting documentation, logical flow of the argument, clarity of the argument, and so on.

While instructors have been using grading rubrics at all levels of higher education for years, they often fail to share the rubric with students before an assignment has begun. As a result, students are judged by standards that were hidden from them. If they had known the expectations from the start of the activity, they would have understood what the expectations were and thus performed at a higher level. (See, for example, Andrade, 2000; Brookhart, 2016; Stevens, Levi, & Walvoord, 2013.)

Colleges and universities can't afford to make the same mistake when it comes to evaluating administrators. Once the list of evaluation criteria has been developed, prioritized, and pared down to the most essential items, it should be shared with the administrator at the *start* of the evaluation period. In fact, the best time to share this list is immediately after the last evaluation. Doing so sends the message, "Here's what you should be working on next, and we're allowing you sufficient time to make progress in these areas."

The vast majority of academic administrators will work diligently to meet the standards that have been set for them. But they can't pursue these goals if they're not shared with them in a timely manner.

Step Eight

Consult with additional experts to improve the process as well as the instruments that will be used for the evaluation.

If you've developed your evaluation subcommittee as recommended earlier, with representation by well-trained members of your school's IRB, you'll already have a process in place that avoids significant problems in the way that many schools gather and interpret appraisal data. But, once your prioritized list of desired behaviors and results has been created and pared down, it's valuable to obtain an external scan of your process and the instruments that you'll use to collect information.

In chapter 1, it was noted that there are a number of companies that specialize in employee evaluation, including those that have a great deal of experience working in higher education. Many of these companies will tailor design an evaluation instrument for you or work with you to adapt one of their existing instruments. Of course, if the firm *doesn't* provide the ability to modify its evaluation form, that's not a company you'll want to use. The goal, as we've seen, is to evaluate this particular administrator at this particular institution at this particular time. Generic evaluation forms won't allow you to do that.

Professional evaluation firms are particularly valuable because they often have regional, national, and perhaps even national data sets to which you can compare administrators at your institution. In that way, you'll have a broader context for interpreting individual scores. Without comparison data, it's impossible to tell whether a score of 3.8 on a 5-point scale in an area like development of external resources is good or bad. But if you discover that the median score of administrators at institutions similar to yours in size and mission was 4.7, you'll have a clearer understanding of what that score means.

If you don't want to use an external form or can't afford one, at least have your process and evaluation forms reviewed by an administrative appraisal committee or IRB at one of your peer institutions. This type of external scan will spot difficulties that even the best people at your own institution are too close to the process to see.

Regardless of whether you hire a professional firm or trade services with a peer institution, make certain that any evaluation instrument you develop adheres to the principles outlined in chapter 1. For example, it should not have more than twelve questions, those questions should be written from the evaluator's own perspective (not the perspective of the administrator or the institution as a whole), and it should use a consistent rating scale.

Step Nine

Gather and analyze information from appropriate stakeholder groups, including the administrator's own self-evaluation.

Once the criteria are established, prioritized, and reviewed, it's possible to begin gathering information relevant to the evaluation. A truly comprehensive performance appraisal will draw on the following sources:

- Properly designed evaluation instruments containing six to twelve multiple-choice questions and one or two open-ended questions completed by representatives from all key stakeholder groups.
- A self-evaluation completed by the administrator that addresses the same performance areas as in the instruments completed by stakeholders.
- An opportunity to create or update an administrative portfolio.
- Additional information obtained through crowdsourcing. (See chapter 1.)

In processes where the stakeholder groups are large enough, it can also be informative to collect demographic information about the respondents. That information will help the subcommittee identify patterns that could be important, such as whether women see themselves as being treated differently from men by the administrator, whether there is a discrepancy in how the administrator interacts with different ethnic groups, whether younger employees have a different experience from older employees, and so on.

A well-trained evaluation subcommittee will need to decide, however, whether the sample size is large enough for this type of demographic analysis. It's impossible for a response to be truly confidential if, for instance, there is only one Asian male in the group who has been at the institution for twenty or more years, and the instrument asks each respondent to state his or her gender, ethnicity, and years of employment.

In addition, small sample sizes can easily skew the results. For example, if 90 percent of the male employees rate the administrator positively but only 5 percent of the female employees respond similarly, that result could mean something quite different depending on the sample size. A group of sixty women whose responses diverge from those of a group of sixty men is almost certainly significant. But if the sample size includes only one woman, it's unclear whether her response in isolation can be regarded as reflecting anything larger than her own individual perceptions.

Remember, too, that when aggregating data from stakeholder groups and analyzing data according to demographic categories, averages calculated as medians and modes are far preferable than averages calculated as arithmetic means. Means, as was explained earlier, are far more affected by outliers—data that deviate substantially from the vast majority of the data—than are medians and modes. That effect is particularly strong when the data set being aggregated is very small.

Step Ten

Have the subcommittee appraise whether the administrator's performance meets the criteria for success that were identified earlier.

When sufficient information has been collected, the evaluation subcommittee should compare those results to the criteria established earlier in order to determine whether the administrator has met expectations in each area. A five-category system (Greatly Exceeds Expectations, Exceeds Expectations, Meets Expectations, Fails to Meet Expectations, and Substantially Fails to Meet Expectations) can help the subcommittee to appraise performance in each area under review.

Unlike the evaluation instruments themselves, however, where all items on a Likert Scale should be spaced in a way that makes each level equidistant from the last, the appraisal categories used at this stage in the process need not (and probably *should* not) be structured in the same way. For example, suppose that one item in the evaluation states, "By the time of the quarterly review, the chancellor will have made progress in implementing the strategic plan by meeting or exceeding at least thirty of the plan's objectives."

The goal shouldn't be that achieving fifty or more objectives will be defined as Greatly Exceeds Expectations, forty as Exceeds Expectations, thirty as Meets Expectations, twenty as Fails to Meet Expectations, and ten or fewer as Substantially Fails to Meet Expectations. There may not even be as many as fifty objectives in the entire plan. Moreover, the target of achieving thirty objectives in the plan by the end of the quarter may have been set as an aspiration, not as a minimal level of satisfactory achievement.

It may well be, therefore, that the scale in this case should be "Achievement of more than thirty objectives constitutes performance that Greatly Exceeds Expectations. Thirty objectives constitute performance that Exceeds Expectations. Twenty-five to twenty-nine goals constitute performance that Meets Expectations. Fifteen to twenty-four goals constitute performance that Fails to Meet Expectations. And accomplishment of fewer than fifteen goals constitutes performance that Substantially Fails to Meet Expectations." The scale in this case is inconsistent, but it is more reasonable than one based on perfectly equidistant categories.

The principle at work here is that the evaluation scale adopted by the supervisory subcommittee should be reasonable and defensible in terms of the performance goals set for the administrator, not some arbitrary standard like equidistance of categories. One of the key reasons for forming the subcommittee in the first place is that it's often necessary to use professional judgment rather than hard and fast rules at various stages in the evaluation process. Developing the standards for appraisal categories is one of the most important of those stages.

The result of this step in the process is to render a summative judgment of the administrator's performance. At some institutions, that judgment will be rendered by the subcommittee itself. At others, the subcommittee will merely be passing a recommendation on to an administrator or group, such as the governing board, that will render the final decision.

Step Eleven

Compare the results of the administrator's self-evaluation to the results provided by stakeholder groups.

Equally important as the results provided by stakeholder groups are the results of the administrator's self-evaluation. In fact, institutions often learn more about a person's performance by comparing the self-evaluation to aggregated scores in the same category of performance. How aware does the administrator seem to be of his or her own strengths and weaknesses? Is the administrator progressing at the same rate that others perceive the administrator to be progressing?

Significant deviation between self-evaluation scores and scores by other administrators indicates two things that should be of concern to the institution. First, it indicates just how unreliable it can be to base a performance appraisal on self-evaluation alone. (This lack of reliability will assume even greater importance when evaluations of the governing board are considered later in this book.)

Second, it provides a useful entrée into sometimes difficult areas. The administrator's supervisor or members of the evaluation subcommittee can begin addressing certain issues by saying, "You rank yourself quite highly in this area, but look at how your performance there is perceived by other stakeholders," or, "You're very hard on yourself when it comes to this area. But I think you can take some pride in how your stakeholders view your performance there."

Step Twelve

Close the loop, part 1: Share the summative judgment with the administrator.

If a summative judgment has arisen from the evaluation, it's only humane to share that result with the administrator as soon as the result has been finalized. When the result is good, the administrator deserves to revel in that positive outcome at the earliest available opportunity. When the result is mixed, he or she deserves to have as much time as possible to build on areas of strength and remediate areas of weakness.

When the result is negative, the administrator will need time to absorb that information and prepare for next steps, which could include looking for a new job.

Examples of possible summative judgments to an administrative evaluation process include the following:

- *Contract status:* The administrator's contract is renewed, terminated, or modified.
- *Compensation:* The administrator is given a merit increase, given a reduction in salary, offered a bonus or deferred compensation, or continued at his or her current level.
- *Commendation:* The administrator is publicly recognized for his or her achievements.
- *Performance plan:* The administrator is required to take certain steps to improve his or her performance.

Many other possibilities exist, but, regardless of what summative judgment is made, it always answers the question, "What decision has been made about the administrator based on his or her past performance?

Step Thirteen

Close the loop, part 2: If appropriate and necessary, offer formative advice to the administrator.

One of the most important results to come out of the evaluation process isn't the summative judgment; it's the formative advice. As was seen earlier, you may discover that the administrator's self-evaluation differs substantially from the results of what other stakeholders report. You may notice assets that the administrator can use to better advantage himself or herself. You may notice weaknesses that can be strengthened. Formative advice serves as the basis for the administrator's continual improvement.

The session(s) in which this information is shared will thus feel much more like a coaching and mentoring opportunity than like a typical performance appraisal meeting. In most cases, the person who shares this information will be the administrator's supervisor. For the president, the board chair, the entire board, or the evaluation subcommittee will probably conduct the meeting.

But no matter who offers this formative advice to the administrator, it's important that the tone of the meeting(s) be constructive, supportive, and forward looking. The basic message should be, "We're not telling you these things because we feel that you've done anything wrong. We're telling them to you because we know you're capable of doing even better and that you're the type of administrator who wants to take advantage of every opportunity to improve."

Step Fourteen

Close the loop, part 3: Inform other stakeholders of the evaluation's results to the extent that is appropriate.

Evaluation procedures fall within the domain of personnel matters. As a result, they frequently involve highly confidential information that only the administrator and those directly involved in the process should know. Nevertheless, stakeholders will want to know whether their insights were taken seriously. They'll want to know that formal decisions have been made and that the process (or at least the current cycle of the process) is at an end.

Informing the stakeholders of the result of the process may consist of nothing more than conveying the message, "Thank you very much for participating in the evaluation of [NAME]. Your insights were very valuable, and we want you to know that they've been carefully considered. Since, however, evaluations are personnel matters, you may not hear anything further about what was reported to the administrator. Nevertheless, be assured that care was taken to preserve the confidentiality of the evaluators and to reach a result that was in the best interest of both the administrator and the institution."

Depending on the situation, there are a number of other possibilities for what stakeholders may be told, including the following:

- "Based on the outcome of the evaluation, [NAME'S] term as [POSITION] will conclude as of [DATE]."
- "Based on the outcome of the evaluation, [NAME'S] term as [POSITION] has been extended until [DATE]."
- "Based on the outcome of the evaluation, we are pleased to commend [NAME] for exceptional service as [POSITION]."

Step Fifteen

Close the loop, part 4: Improve the process for next time.

A good evaluation process results in advice on how to improve not only the administrator's performance but also the evaluation process itself. Were there questions on the evaluation instrument that were unclear either to the administrator or to others participating in the evaluation? Were there concerns about the confidentiality of the information provided that need to be addressed during further iterations? Were there areas of performance that the evaluation subcommittee or the administrator's supervisor particularly cared about that couldn't be addressed during the current process?

The formative advice emerging from the evaluation also provides the possibility for setting goals and targets that will be appraised during the administrator's *next* evaluation. To whatever extent possible, these goals should be structured according to the template provided earlier. For example, if a provost was regarded as acting too autocratically and failing to consult with others, a goal similar to the following might be created.

> By the date of the next quarterly review, the provost will have demonstrated improvement in the area of consultation by conferring with the Council of Deans about at least two of the policy changes recommended in the strategic plan for the Division of Academic Affairs, soliciting the advice of the deans, and achieving consensus about how the policy should be modified.

STREAMLINING THE PROCESS

Admittedly any fifteen-step process is likely to appear cumbersome and overly complicated to those who have to implement it. Nevertheless, it should be recognized that the process recommended here has been broken down into numerous steps for the purpose of avoiding the pitfalls commonly made in administrative evaluations. In actual practice, many steps in this process occur simultaneously (or nearly so), and so the evaluation of administrators can actually be viewed as a more streamlined process consisting of these elements:

1. *Preparing for the evaluation:* Steps one through eight.
2. *Conducting the evaluation:* Steps nine through eleven.
3. *Concluding the evaluation:* Steps twelve through fifteen.

CONCLUSION

Many systems for evaluating administrators are not as effective as they could be because they fail to implement all the steps included in the *Preparing the Evaluation* section just mentioned. The assumption made at these institutions is often, "We know what the critical functions of a position are because we've developed a formal job description for each position."

But job descriptions are not reliable sources of information about an administrator's most critical functions. Those functions evolve over time, while the job descriptions themselves are rarely updated. Moreover, as all administrators soon learn, "There's what it says I do on paper, and there's what I actually do." Good administrators create their own "job descriptions" over time by stretching themselves and the units they supervise in ways that could not have been anticipated when they were appointed to their positions.

In addition, what administrators do can vary considerably from one school to the next or even from one division to the next within the same institution. The president of a large research university has very different responsibilities from the president of a small church-affiliated college or a two-year community college. What constitutes success for a provost is very different from what constitutes success for the vice president for student affairs or the vice president for business affairs. As a result, meaningful evaluation for college administrators must begin with the questions, "What does this person actually do for the institution?" and, "How best can we objectively measure success in those areas?"

KEY POINTS IN THIS CHAPTER

Effective evaluation of administrators consists of the following process:
A. *Preparing for the evaluation*
   1. Identify the group that is most appropriate for supervising the evaluation process.
   2. Have the supervisory subcommittee supervise the process of determining the most critical functions of each position being evaluated.
   3. Describe specific behaviors or results that constitute success in each of the key functions that have been identified.
   4. Rank the specific behaviors or results that constitute success in order of priority.
   5. Identify objective and reliable sources of information about those specific behaviors and results.
   6. Pare the specific behaviors or results that constitute success down to a reasonable number.
   7. Communicate these criteria to the administrator at the start of the evaluation period.
   8. Consult with additional experts to improve the process as well as the instruments that will be used for the evaluation.
B. *Conducting the evaluation*
   9. Gather and analyze information from appropriate stakeholder groups, including the administrator's own self-evaluation.

10. Have the subcommittee appraise whether the administrator's performance meets the criteria for success that were identified earlier.
   11. Compare the results of the administrator's self-evaluation to the results provided by stakeholder groups.

C. Concluding the evaluation

   12. Close the loop, part 1: Share the summative judgment with the administrator.
   13. Close the loop, part 2: If appropriate and necessary, offer formative advice to the administrator.
   14. Close the loop, part 3: Inform other stakeholders of the evaluation's results to the extent that is appropriate.
   15. Close the loop, part 4: Improve the process for next time.

REFERENCES

Andrade, H. G. 2000. Using Rubrics to promote thinking and learning. *Educational Leadership, 57,* 13–19.

Brookhart, S. M. 2016. *How to create and use rubrics for formative assessment and grading.* Alexandria, VA: ACSD.

Buller, J. 2012. *The essential department chair: A comprehensive desk reference* (2nd ed.). San Francisco, CA: Jossey-Bass.

Seldin, P., & Miller, J. E. 2009. *The academic portfolio: A practical guide to documenting teaching, research, and service.* San Francisco, CA: Jossey-Bass.

Seldin, P., Miller, J. E., & C. A. Seldin, C. A. 2010. *The teaching portfolio: A practical guide to improved performance and promotion/tenure decisions* (4th ed.). San Francisco: Jossey-Bass.

Stevens, D. D., A. Levi, & Walvoord, B. E. F. 2013. *Introduction to rubrics: An assessment tool to save grading time, convey effective feedback, and promote student learning* (6th ed.). Sterling, VA: Stylus.

St. Charles Community College. 2019. Responsibilities of the college president. https://www.stchas.edu/about-scc/administration/board-policies/112-Responsibilities-of-the-College-President.

University of New Mexico. 2016. Regents' policy manual—Section 3.1: Responsibilities of the president. https://policy.unm.edu/regents-policies/section-3/3-1.html.

RESOURCES

Antony, J. S., Cauce, A. M., & Shalala, D. E. 2017. *Challenges in higher education leadership: practical and scholarly solutions.* New York, NY: Routledge.
Bahrman, D. 2011. *Evaluating and improving organizational governance.* Altamonte Springs, FL: The Institute of Internal Auditors Research Foundation.
Buller, J. L. 2015. *The essential academic dean or provost: A comprehensive desk reference* (2nd ed.). San Francisco, CA: Jossey-Bass.
Martin, J. 2015. *Provost's handbook.* Baltimore, MD: Johns Hopkins University Press.
Nielsen, L. A. 2019. *Provost: Experiences, reflections, and advice from a former "number two" on campus.* Sterling, VA: Stylus.
Sternberg, R. J. (ed.). 2015. *Academic leadership in higher education: From the top down and the bottom up.* Lanham, MD: Rowman & Littlefield.
Trachtenberg, S. J., Kauvar, G. B., & Gee, E. G. (eds.). 2018. *Leading colleges and universities: Lessons from higher education leaders.* Baltimore, MD: Johns Hopkins University Press.

3

BEST PRACTICES IN ADMINISTRATIVE EVALUATIONS

An important objection might be raised about the process for administrative evaluation that was recommended in the last chapter: "It's all well and good to argue that this is how administrators *should* be evaluated, but our institution already has policies specifying how administrators *must* be evaluated." Indeed, in many cases, those policies have been mandated by accrediting bodies, governing boards, or even legislatures and can't be easily modified.

This objection raises a valid point, but there's a practice dated to at least the time of Plato and Aristotle that says, whenever you're trying to improve anything, start first by envisioning *the best that is possible* and then derive from that concept *the best that is practical*. Or to use a different metaphor, "Play by the rules you have until you're in a position to write the rules you need."

It may not be realistic, therefore, for many colleges and universities to move immediately to the system of administrative evaluation that was described in chapter 2. But there are many colleges and universities that already have excellent policies for evaluating administrators, and it may be possible to borrow from them some of their effective practices even if your institution is not yet in a position to create the evaluation system it would ultimately like to have.

RECOMMENDATIONS FROM THE AMERICAN ASSOCIATION OF UNIVERSITY PROFESSORS

For example, the American Association of University Professors (AAUP) has articulated a number of specific recommendations about what the role of the professoriate should be in the evaluation of administrators. Because of the influence the AAUP has in higher education, it may be possible to use this group's guidelines to bring about meaningful change at your institution.

Here are a number of AAUP recommendations that colleges and universities should consider when evaluating key administrators.

- Because the design and implementation of an institution's curriculum is a responsibility entrusted to the faculty, "The faculty role in the evaluation of administrators [should] be especially focused on faculty interaction with administrators directly charged with the oversight of the educational program, of students, and of such personnel matters as salaries, promotion, and tenure" (Faculty Evaluation of Administrators, n.d.).
- "The most effective systems of administrator evaluation are those that occur *periodically* as part of a *collaborative* endeavor involving the faculty, the administration, other campus constituencies with a stake in the outcome, and the individual under review" (Faculty Evaluation of Administrators, n.d.). In other words, administrative evaluation should be conducted regularly, not used as a tool for remediation only when problems have arisen.
- Administrators should not be evaluated solely by their supervisors because they make decisions that affect many more stakeholder groups than their supervisors alone. "Faculty participation in the evaluation of a president or other chief executive officer, such as a chancellor, is . . . conditioned on that person's role as an institutional leader and spokesperson but should recognize that other constituencies—students, staff, alumni, and, in terms of ultimate authority as well as delegation of responsibilities, the board of

- trustees—have equally important roles to play" (Faculty Evaluation of Administrators, n.d.).
- Faculty members should be informed as to the outcome of an administrative evaluation.
- "In general, a distinction should be made between *annual reappointment reviews*, which might be quite swift and of a lesser degree of formality, intended mainly for purposes of constructive suggestions about the administrator's performance, and a *comprehensive end-of-term review*, in which non-reappointment to the administrative post is a possible outcome" (Faculty Evaluation of Administrators, n.d.).
- The suggestions on improving performance that arise from an annual reappointment review should, in general, be kept confidential so that the administrator can use this information as a basis for improvement with undue embarrassment. The outcome of a comprehensive end-of-term review should, however, be made public.
- Even if there is a subcommittee that supervises the evaluation process as recommended in Chapter 1, the AAUP recommends that there also be a separate committee "composed entirely of faculty members . . . [so that it can] reach distinct faculty recommendations." Indeed, "The degree of faculty participation should be appropriate to the nature of the administrative office whose holder is under review." The AAUP also notes that "An effective way of ensuring as wide a spectrum of faculty participation as desired by the faculty is the development of a questionnaire" (Faculty Evaluation of Administrators, n.d.).
- Among the criteria for evaluating chief executive officers, the AAUP recommends "interaction with faculty, interaction with students, interaction with the community, management of administrative units, . . . leadership, . . . securing funds for faculty compensation and new faculty recruitment, promoting the value of research to the external public, effectively supporting teaching and service to that same public, . . . demonstrating commitment to

diversity, clarity of strategic goals, and effectiveness in appointing efficient and responsible campus administrators" (Faculty Evaluation of Administrators, n.d.).

One of the conclusions made in the AAUP's discussion of administrator review by faculty members is that "the review should, as far as possible, be constructive and provide the supervising administrator or body with adequate grounds for reaching an informed decision when continuance of the person being reviewed is at stake" (Faculty Evaluation of Administrators, n.d.). In other words, the goal of administrative evaluation should not be to intensify the often adversarial relationship between faculty members and administrators but rather to form a partnership based on the best principles of shared governance that allows each group to help increase the effectiveness of the other.

GEORGIA COLLEGE AND STATE UNIVERSITY

One useful way of understanding how the AAUP's recommendations on evaluation of administrators (as well as other best practices) can be used to improve performance is to examine the actual policies of several institutions, particularly those that align well with AAUP guidelines. Georgia College and State University (GCSU) in Milledgeville, the city that served as the capital of Georgia during the Civil War, has developed an approach based on requirements set by the state's *Board of Regents Policy Manual* but that also goes beyond those requirements to reflect the institution's mission as the state's designated public liberal arts university and that incorporates, either by intention or coincidence, many of the best practices advocated by the AAUP.

GCSU's policy states that, although administrative evaluation can be used as a basis for deciding whether an academic leader should be retained, its primary purpose is "to provide a systematic means of recognizing and documenting the significant administrative work of those evaluated, provide a continuing comment on administrative performance, and encourage an academic administration that is responsive to the mission of the college including both teaching environment and professional development of faculty and staff" (Performance Evaluations for Academic Administrators, n.d.). From the very beginning of its policy, therefore, the university makes it clear that its goal is to recognize and document achievement, not merely to penalize or improve substandard performance.

The following are some of the other best practices included in the administrative review policy developed by GCSU:

- It is clearly stated that administrative evaluation relates only to the person's performance *as an administrator*. If he or she also holds academic rank, that person's performance in teaching, research, and service will be evaluated by means of the same procedure used to evaluate any other faculty member. As a way of emphasizing this point, the policy notes that "Administrators do not hold tenure with respect to administrative positions; tenure may be awarded for faculty rank only" (Performance Evaluations for Academic Administrators, n.d.).
- All administrators must be evaluated by their supervisors at least once a year. "Specific evaluations may occur at any time unusual administrative performance, circumstances, or accomplishments warrant" (Performance Evaluations for Academic Administrators, n.d.). Moreover, there will be an especially thorough evaluation of the administrator every five years in accordance with state system guidelines.
- The evaluation is tied to the administrator's specific duties rather than to administration or leadership in general.
- The evaluation is further tied to any specific goals that were established for the administrator during the evaluation period.
- Both a self-evaluation and an evaluation based on observations provided by the administrator's main constituencies are conducted as part of the process. "All faculty have the opportunity to participate in the evaluation of the academic administrators" (Performance Evaluations for Academic Administrators, n.d.). The provost takes the lead in communicating with other institutional

stakeholders, advising them that they have an opportunity to participate in the evaluation of academic administrators.
- The administrator's overall performance evaluation and the recommendation for his or her reappointment must be reviewed and approved by the administrator's supervisor.

THE STATE UNIVERSITY OF NEW YORK

In 2005, a report on the faculty evaluation of administrators was submitted to the University Faculty Senate of the State University of New York (SUNY) by that body's Governance Committee. The report was prompted by several concerns. First, although the university's chancellor had initiated a process of regular evaluation of campus presidents, local faculty members felt that they had very little ownership of that process.

The annual review process conducted by the chancellor did not require a faculty role, although periodic full-scale evaluation of campus presidents—typically conducted after three years for new presidents and every five years for continuing presidents—*did* solicit faculty involvement. Furthermore, the chancellors' guidelines required that "requests for comments regarding Presidential stewardship shall be considered confidential" (Faculty Evaluation of Administrators, 2005).

Second, faculty members at the university believed that the need for accountability and transparency throughout the institution required that *line review* (i.e., evaluation by one's supervisor for the purposes of determining continuation and merit) should be complemented by 360-degree review for the purposes of formative evaluation.

Third, when the Governance Committee conducted a survey of all twenty-seven campuses within the SUNY System in 2003–2004, it was discovered that "just over half [of the twenty-four institutions responding to the survey] indicated that guidelines for evaluation were 'in place,' but a large majority of campuses reported that there was 'little or no role for faculty governance in evaluation of senior administrators.' . . . [Thus,] while guidelines may be in place, they are often not implemented on a regular basis or at all" (Faculty Evaluation of Administrators, 2005).

Among the best practices included in the report released by the Governance Committee of SUNY's University Faculty Senate, it is important to note the following:

- Evaluation of administrators is expected to follow a process that is fair, consistent, constructive, and as forward looking as possible. "While administrators under review may not always be eager to embrace evaluation, they will accept it more readily when they perceive that the process is being administered fairly and that results generated are used to improve job performance" (Faculty Evaluation of Administrators, 2005).
- The evaluation committee should represent all constituencies affected by decisions that the administrator makes.
- Just as faculty members are typically reviewed in their first year of service, waiting until the third year of an administrator's service is too long. Issues that are initially minor can become serious problems if left unaddressed.
- Use of standardized evaluation instruments promotes consistency. Use of locally developed evaluation instruments reflects the distinctive opportunities and challenges of the institution's specific environment. Therefore, it was recommended that evaluation instruments should combine standardized items with items that are "custom tailored" for that particular administrator.
- Those who participate in the evaluation process by completing surveys or supplying information should be informed of key results at the end of the process, "even if it is only an edited summary" (Faculty Evaluation of Administrators, 2005).

In June 2013, the Governance Committee issued a handbook that contained additional recommendations and policies on the evaluation of administrators. In this subsequent document, it was recommended that the process of evaluating campus presidents should last approximately six to eight weeks (excluding periods when the university was not in session) from the chancellor's initiation of the process until the chancellor's visit to the institution to complete the process. That time frame would allow adequate time for participants to be notified of the process and to make thorough, well-considered responses.

It was further recommended that the president's self-evaluation be shared with the faculty governance leaders at the institution and that, at the conclusion of the process, "The results of the evaluation and the meeting with the Chancellor should be reported to the faculty governance executive committee and to the campus community" (*Governance Handbook*, 2013, p. 83).

SOUTHEASTERN LOUISIANA UNIVERSITY

The document titled *Policy and Procedures for the Evaluation of the President and Vice Presidents* at Southeastern Louisiana University (SLU) opens with what might be regarded as a model statement about how performance reviews of senior administrators benefit an institution.

For example, the document notes that the reasons why administrators are regularly evaluated is that administrative review promotes accountability, provides an opportunity for an institution to judge the performance of its leaders within the context of the school's mission and vision, helps support effective leadership, reduces capricious judgments of administrators by using a systematic and consistent process, and gives the university a valuable means to check its progress toward various goals (*Policy and Procedures for the Evaluation of the President and Vice Presidents*, 1997, pp. 1–2).

SLU's policy also spells out the institutional values that are intended to guide its evaluation process. Specifically, the document states that SLU is dedicated to evaluating key administrators in a manner that is *objective*, based on clearly described *criteria* that the administrator is aware of well in advance of the evaluation, *meaningful* in that it reflects the observations of people who have worked closely enough with senior administrators to have witnessed their performance, and conducted in accordance with a reasonable *timetable*.

The policy also specifies how the information collected during the evaluation is to be reported (and to whom), requires that the administrator being evaluated have an opportunity for self-evaluation and to respond to the criticism of others, and establishes that the review process itself will be evaluated periodically in order to make sure that it remains valuable despite changes at the institution (*Policy and Procedures for the Evaluation of the President and Vice Presidents*, 1997, pp. 3–4).

Among the other best practices included in SLU's evaluation procedure are the following:

- The composition of the presidential review committee is quite broad, including a member of the faculty (the faculty senate president), two midlevel academic leaders (the chair of the department heads council and a representative of the deans council), a direct report (a representative of the vice presidents), a student (the student government association president), and a member of the community (the chair of the president's community advisory committee).
- An even broader set of stakeholders is allowed to participate actively in the review through submission of standardized evaluation forms. For example, evaluation forms are made available to unclassified employees (such as directors and those with the word *assistant* in their titles), as well as representatives from the alumni association board and foundation board.
- At the conclusion of the evaluation process, the president meets with the presidential review committee to discuss the degree to which he or she has attained this year's goals and how well his or her actions have aligned with the university's strategic plan.
- The result of the evaluation is filed annually with the office of institutional research and assessment.
- For vice presidents, evaluation forms combine standardized questions with as many as five additional questions that deal with the

specific roles and functions of that administrator. These added questions are agreed upon in advance by both the president and the vice president who is being evaluated.
- As with the president, appropriately broad constituencies evaluate each vice president.
- At the close of the review process for vice presidents, the president discusses the results of the evaluation with the person who has been reviewed and places a summary report in that vice president's personnel file.

TEXAS WOMEN'S UNIVERSITY

In the same year that SUNY's governance committee issued its handbook, Texas Women's University (TWU) developed a revised set of policies and procedures for the evaluation of its administrators. A review process had been approved by TWU's board of regents as early as 1994, but the 2013 document helped to clarify and systematize the procedures that were by then in common use at the university.

The document grounds the process of evaluating administrators on the institution's commitment to accountability and notes that formal review of academic leaders is required by the school's regional accreditor, the Southern Association of Colleges and Schools Commission on Colleges. The TWU policy states that "the purpose of providing information to administrators about their performance is to promote their personal, professional, and administrative growth and development" (Administrator Evaluations Task Force, 2013, p. 2). Like GCSU and SUNY, therefore, TWU regards its policy as primarily formative, with the goal of eliminating ineffective administrators as only a secondary concern.

The policy developed by TWU promotes transparency by specifying precisely which administrators are to be evaluated, beginning with the chancellor and president and continuing down to the level of department chairs, program directors, and their assistants or associates. It notes that the process used at the university "will assess faculty perceptions of an administrator's performance in three general areas: (1) leadership and decision-making skills, (2) organizational skills and administrative methods, and (3) personal characteristics" (Administrator Evaluations Task Force, 2013, p. 3).

Among the other best practices included in TWU's Administrator Evaluation Process (AEP) are the following:

- The policy outlines specific criteria to be used in administrative evaluations. For example, in evaluation of the president and chancellor, provost, and individual academic units, evaluations of twenty-one different criteria are mentioned, such as clarity of strategic goals, success in creating a sense of unity, civility, and purpose, commitment to diversity, establishing good relations with faculty and students, and securing funds for faculty compensation and new faculty recruitment.
- The criteria selected for each evaluation should be "tailored for the individual administrator . . . [and should] account for aspects of job performance that are specific to a particular position or services rendered by a specific administrative unit" (Administrator Evaluations Task Force, 2013, p. 5).
- The administrators being evaluated are given an opportunity to provide additional questions to be used as part of the instrument distributed to their stakeholders during performance reviews.
- These instruments must contain a mixture of quantitative and open-ended questions and be distributed both in paper format and online.
- Faculty participation in the review process isn't limited just to full-time faculty but is open to any faculty member with a 50 percent or higher FTE (full-time equivalent) position. The administrator being evaluated also has the option to extend the evaluation pool to adjuncts with less than a 50 percent FTE position, graduate teaching assistants, or both.
- While quantitative results are sent to the administrator's supervisor, qualitative results will be sent only to the administrator being

evaluated. In this way, the answers to open-ended questions remain purely formative in nature.
- These quantitative results are also shared with the administrators, the faculty senate executive committee, and the general assembly of the faculty senate, ensuring that the process is as transparent as possible.
- The office of technology provides assistance when numerical results are reviewed as a way of making certain that statistically insignificant findings don't skew the results.
- The evaluation process begins with an administrator's first year of service and is conducted every two or three years after that, depending on length of service. In this way, if any problems exist, they can be addressed early in an administrator's tenure before they become truly severe.
- After the results have been processed, it is strongly recommended that two meetings take place, one with the administrator and his or her supervisor and the other with the administrator and the faculty. The topics to be discussed in these meetings may include goals that were achieved, factors that prevented goals from being achieved, areas of concern about the administrator's performance that were raised during the evaluation process, and future objectives.

Despite this long list of excellent practices seen in the TWU process, one aspect of the university's policy may cause concern at some institutions. The evaluation procedure specifically excludes administrators holding interim positions. That exclusion deprives acting administrators from receiving the formative benefits that can result from the review process. It also ignores the fact that colleges and universities do occasionally suffer serious harm when the performance of administrators holding interim positions is not subject to 360-degree evaluation.

BEST PRACTICES IN DEVELOPING EVALUATION INSTRUMENTS

The vast majority of instruments or surveys currently in use for evaluating administrators are far too long. For example, a chancellor evaluation form developed by the Southern University System in 2011 asks participants to rate the CEO on forty-five separate items (see Chancellor Evaluation Form, 2011). A sample form drafted by the Association of Community College Trustees (ACCT) contains fifty-seven (!) separate items (see Sample Presidential Performance Appraisal, n.d.).

As was indicated in chapter 1, instruments that include more than twelve items tend to encourage the halo effect at best and to discourage completion at worst. People who are completing the forms either give up entirely or stop reading each question carefully and start answering all questions in the same way, based merely on whether their overall impression of the administrator is positive or negative.

Long instruments also often suffer from the flaws of not being phrased from the perspective of the observer and of assuming that the observer can provide insights into aspects of the administrator's performance that he or she hasn't witnessed firsthand. For example, one item on the Southern University System survey mentioned above states, "Based upon the chancellor's leadership, faculty and staff have confidence in the future of the university" (Chancellor Evaluation Form, 2011).

No observer can speak authoritatively on behalf of the entire faculty and staff. It would be far better to say, "Based upon the chancellor's leadership, I have confidence in the future of the university," or "My impression is that my peers have confidence in the future of the university due to the chancellor's leadership." In this way, the observers are answering the question from their own experience. Then, by cross-tabulating the responses to the item with demographic information, the supervising subcommittee can more accurately gauge whether certain patterns emerge among the faculty, staff, or both.

Similarly, on the instrument proposed by the ACCT, respondents (who are presumed to be governing board members) are asked whether the president is informed about developments in education. If board members themselves aren't informed about those developments—and they may well not be because they work in industry, government, or other fields and not in higher education—they're not in an appropriate position to answer this question.

In addition, many items on the ACCT form are compound rather than focused. For example, one item states, "Technology is continuously upgraded and used as a tool to promote greater student access, learning options, service, efficiencies and productivity" (Sample Presidential Performance Appraisal, n.d.). If technology is indeed continually upgraded but not used as a tool for any of the purposes mentioned, how should the respondent answer this question? Or what should the respondent do if technology is upgraded but only used as a tool to promote the first two goals but not the last three?

In order for the information gained from a survey about administrative performance to be meaningful, the instrument should consist of a carefully selected set of six to twelve items that are highly relevant to the administrator's specific duties and current goals and based on what the respondent has personally observed. Different instruments should thus be written for different stakeholder groups because those groups will vary in both expertise and vantage point. "I was able to converse with the chancellor informally at such locations at the food court, my residence hall, or the student union" is a suitable item on an instrument intended for students but not the chancellor's peers. "I consider the chancellor to be well-regarded among other college or university CEOs" is a suitable item on an instrument intended for other upper-level administrators but not for students.

The following set of suggested items is not intended, therefore, to serve as an evaluation survey that is used in its entirety. Rather, it is a master set of potential items from which an appropriate subset should be selected for individual instruments.

Leadership

- I am aware of the administrator's vision for the future, regardless of whether I personally agree with all aspects of that vision.
- I believe that the administrator has a strategy for achieving his or her vision for the future.
- I have confidence in the administrator's leadership.
- When this administrator says something, I believe that I trust it.
- I feel that the administrator is aware of the issues that concern me.
- I feel that the administrator cares about the issues that concern me.
- I have reason to believe that the administrator values perspectives other than his or her own.
- I believe that the administrator fosters an environment that encourages the free exchange of ideas.
- I believe that the administrator gathers pertinent information before acting.
- I believe that the administrator accepts responsibility when it is appropriate to do so.
- In my experience, the administrator makes timely decisions.
- In my experience, the administrator makes reasonable decisions.
- In my experience, the administrator is willing to explain decisions that he or she has made.

Communication

- In my experience, the administrator has been visible at important public events.
- In my experience, the administrator communicates with others in a timely manner.
- In my experience, the administrator communicates with others in a collegial manner.
- In my experience, the administrator provides accurate information when communicating.
- In my experience, the administrator speaks clearly.

- In my experience, the administrator speaks concisely.
- In my experience, the administrator accepts constructive criticism.

Learning Environment

- I believe that the administrator actively promotes an environment that supports excellence in teaching.
- I believe that the administrator supports high standards in teaching and learning.
- In my experience, the administrator monitors courses in order to make certain that enrollments are at suitable levels.
- In my experience, the administrator supports curricular development.
- In my experience, the administrator supports curricular revision when needed.
- In my experience, the administrator effectively addresses issues of class scheduling.

Institutional Environment

- In my experience, the administrator promotes an environment that supports excellence in research.
- In my experience, the administrator promotes an environment that supports excellence in institutional service.
- I believe that the administrator is properly attentive to issues of safety.

Budgeting

- In my experience, the administrator has a good sense of the overall budget of the institution/program.
- I believe that the administrator manages budgets effectively.
- I believe that the administrator is an effective steward of the program's/institution's resources.

- In my experience, the administrator has been successful in increasing the program's resources.

Administration

- In my experience, the administrator acts as an effective liaison between the program and the broader community.
- In my experience, the administrator conducts meetings effectively.
- In my experience, the administrator holds an appropriate number of meetings.
- In my experience, the administrator is readily accessible for consultation.
- In my experience, the administrator is collegial.
- In my experience, I have found the administrator to be well organized.
- I believe that the administrator is appropriately attentive to matters of diversity.
- In my experience, the administrator's demeanor is properly professional.
- I believe that the administrator promotes inclusiveness in the activities of the institution.
- In my experience, the facilities under this administrator's supervision are properly maintained.
- In my experience, the equipment under this administrator's supervision is properly maintained.
- I believe that the administrator provides for effective long-range planning.
- I believe that the administrator follows through on commitments to the extent possible.
- I believe that the administrator applies policies fairly.
- In academic areas, I believe that the administrator supports development of innovative programs.
- In nonacademic areas, I believe that the administrator supports development of innovative programs.

- In my experience, the administrator effectively manages day-to-day operations of the areas he or she supervises.
- I believe that the administrator is appropriately involved in community activities.

Mentoring and Evaluation

- In my experience, the administrator serves as a good role model or mentor for others.
- In my experience, the administrator helps others set their professional goals.
- In my experience, the administrator helps others achieve their professional goals.
- In my experience, the administrator rewards performance consistent with established expectations.
- In my experience, the administrator evaluates others fairly.
- In my experience, the administrator expresses appreciation to others for their accomplishments.

Open-Ended Items

- If you wish to explain your answer to any of the above items, please do so in the space below.
- Is there anything you wish we'd ask you but didn't? If so, please supply what you'd like to tell us in the space below.

Demographic Information

Relationship to the Institution
- ☐ Administrator
- ☐ Full-time faculty
- ☐ Part-time faculty
- ☐ Staff

☐ Student
☐ Community member
☐ Board member
☐ Other
☐ Prefer not to say

Gender

☐ Male
☐ Female
☐ Mixed gender, transitioning, exploring, or otherwise neither of the above
☐ Prefer not to say

Ethnicity

☐ White/Caucasian/European American
☐ Black/African/African American
☐ Latinx/Latino/Chicano/Hispanic
☐ Asian
☐ Native American/American Indian
☐ Multicultural/Blended heritage
☐ Other
☐ Prefer not to say

How many years have you been associated with this institution? _____ year(s)

Although the goal is to create an evaluation instrument that includes only a small subset of the questions about what the respondent believes or has experienced, it is strongly recommended that the form contain the entirety of the sections headed *Open-ended Items* and *Demographic Information*. As was stated in chapter 1, it's just as bad to include too many open-item questions as it is to include none at all. An item such as "If you wish to explain your answer to any of the above items, please do so in the space below" allows the respondent to clarify answers that would otherwise be unclear.

For example, if the item "The administrator is appropriately involved in community activities" is included on the survey, people may respond positively or negatively for a variety of reasons. The respondent might give a low score to the administrator out of a belief that the person engages in *too many* community activities, *too few* community activities, or *the wrong kind* of community activities.

In fact, the question was phrased as broadly as possible precisely so that the reviewer could interpret it however he or she wished. But by providing an opportunity to explain any answer on the form, a survey allows the respondent to clarify what he or she had in mind when indicating that the administrator's involvement in the community was somehow inappropriate.

In the demographic section of evaluation forms, many institutions provide either too few choices (such as limiting the choices of gender to male or female) or too many (such as providing every imaginable possibility for administrative assignments). Issues of gender and ethnic identity are becoming increasingly complex, and the goal should not be to make any respondent feel disenfranchised by the way the instrument is phrased.

At the same time, providing too many choices in certain categories makes it easy for people to identify individual respondents even when they submit their forms anonymously. For example, there may be only one female and multiracial senior vice president who has worked at the institution for more than ten years. She wouldn't have to sign the form for her identity to be obvious from the demographic information alone.

For this reason, unless it's vitally important to determine whether senior vice presidents (or even all vice presidents) had a significantly different experience from deans, directors, and department chairs, it's better on evaluation forms to have fewer administrative categories in the demographic section than more.

In the best of all possible worlds, of course, the question about the respondent's relationship to the institution can be omitted entirely. If the instruments have been properly designed so that administrators, full-time faculty members, part-time faculty members, staff members, students, community members, board members, and other stakeholders each receive a customized form that includes perhaps three or four questions that are asked of everyone along with perhaps four or five questions that are specifically tailored to the interests of that constituency, it is unnecessary to ask the respondent to indicate his or her relationship to the institution. The version of the form itself will provide that information.

CONCLUSION

When institutions set out to establish or revise a policy on how best to evaluate administrators, they often make the false assumption that they need to start from scratch. There are actually many examples of excellent policies in existence, and these policies can easily be adapted to fit the specific mission, needs, and goals of any institution.

Despite how common good evaluation policies are (a representative sample of which were discussed in this chapter), it's also unfortunately true that a large number of poor policies also exist. Many institutions conduct evaluations by involving only the administrator's supervisor or, in the case of the CEO, the governing board. They rely on evaluation instruments that are poorly designed, often because these forms are far too long or contain ill-conceived questions. Other institutions evaluate administrators only when a problem arises, thus missing out on the opportunity to make administrative review a truly constructive and forward-looking process that is part of its regular procedures.

If you're looking for examples of good policies to use as models, therefore, ask yourself the following questions. Is the policy comprehensive enough to provide a complete picture of the administrator's performance? Does it ask the right questions of the right stakeholders? Have quantitative items and how the results of these quantitative items are tabulated been reviewed by experts in questionnaire design and statistical analysis? Are appropriate stakeholder groups informed of the results of the evaluation when the process has been completed? Does the evaluation process help the administrator set goals and measure his or her progress in reaching those goals?

KEY POINTS IN THIS CHAPTER

Of the many examples of good evaluation practices outlined in this chapter, the following should be considered the most important.

- Administrative evaluation should not be performed solely by the person's supervisor or by the governing board. Every stakeholder group that is affected by the administrator's decisions should be included when information is gathered about the administrator's performance.
- The review process should also require the administrator to perform a self-evaluation.
- Administrative evaluation should review a person's performance *solely as an administrator*. If the administrator holds academic rank in addition to his or her leadership duties, performance in teaching, research, and service should be evaluated in accordance with the same policies used to evaluate any other faculty member.
- The focus of the evaluation should be on the administrator's *specific* duties rather than on administration or leadership in general.
- The administrators being evaluated should have an opportunity, whenever possible, to provide additional questions to the instrument used during their reviews.
- When the administrator is informed of the results of the evaluation, he or she should have an opportunity to respond to it and to assist in setting goals for the next evaluation period.
- Demographic questions on evaluation instruments should help the institution determine whether any group has a significantly different experience of the administrator's performance from that of other groups.

- Demographic questions should not, however, be so numerous or so specific that it becomes possible to identify individual respondents on the basis of these questions alone.

REFERENCES

Administrator Evaluations Task Force. (2013). *Guidelines and procedures for the TWU Administrator Evaluation Process (AEP) by faculty.* https://twu.edu/media/documents/faculty-senate/July_2013_Guidelines_for_Faculty_Senate_Administrator_Eva.pdf.

Chancellor Evaluation Form: Southern University System. (2011). http://www.sus.edu/assets/sus/Administration/Evaluations/chancellorevaluationform-2011.pdf.

Faculty Evaluation of Administrators: American Association of University Professors. (n.d.). https://www.aaup.org/report/faculty-evaluation-administrators.

Faculty Evaluation of Administrators: State University of New York. (2005). https://system.suny.edu/media/suny/content-assets/documents/faculty-senate/FacultyEvaluation.pdf.

Governance Committee of the University Faculty Senate, *Governance Handbook*, State University of New York. (2013). https://system.suny.edu/media/suny/content-assets/documents/faculty-senate/GovHandbook-Final-2013.pdf.

Performance Evaluations for Academic Administrators: Georgia College and State University. (n.d.) https://gcsu.smartcatalogiq.com/en/Policy-Manual/Policy-Manual/Academic-Affairs/EmploymentPolicies-Procedures-Benefits/Performance-Evaluations-Administrators-and-Faculty/Performance-Evaluations-for-Academic-Administrators.

Policy and Procedures for the Evaluation of the President and Vice Presidents: Southeastern Louisiana University. (1997). https://www.southeastern.edu/admin/ir/inst_eff/files/admin_eval_policy.pdf.

Sample Presidential Performance Appraisal: Association of Community College Trustees. (n.d.) http://districtboards.org/documents/Quarterly%20Meeting/714/ACCTSample%20Pres%20Evaluation%20DRAFT.pdf.

RESOURCES

American Council of Trustees and Alumni (n.d.). *Assessing the President's Performance: A "How to" Guide for Trustees.* https://www.goacta.org/images/download/assessing_the_presidents_performance.pdf.

Heck, R. H., Johnsrud, L. K., & Rosser, V. J. (2000). Administrative effectiveness in higher education: Improving assessment procedures. *Research in Higher Education: Journal of the Association for Institutional Research, 41*(6), 663–84.

How Presidential Evaluations Must Change. (2002). *Association of Governing Boards.* https://agb.org/trusteeship-article/how-presidential-evaluations-must-change/.

McKerrow, K. K., & Dennis, L. J. (1989). Evaluation of university presidents: Broadening the perspective. *The Journal of Educational Thought/Revue De La Pensée Éducative, 23*(1), 3–14.

Miller, D. S. (1993). *Evaluating Administrators: Designing the Process in a Shared Governance Environment.* Washington, DC: ERIC Clearinghouse.

4

HOW TO EVALUATE BOARDS EFFECTIVELY

In chapter 1, we saw that more and more accrediting bodies like the Northwest Commission on Colleges and Universities (NWCCU), the Accrediting Commission for Community and Junior Colleges of the Western Association of Schools and College (ACCJC), and the Southern Association of Colleges and Schools Commission on Colleges (SAC-SCOC) are requiring that governing boards be evaluated regularly. But meeting this requirement often requires overcoming even more challenges than are found when conducting administrative evaluations.

First, since governing boards typically occupy the highest rank in an institution's hierarchy, true 360-degree evaluation isn't possible. There is no one who can serve as the board's "supervisor" in providing the top-down component of a 360-degree evaluation. Moreover, even peer evaluation is challenging when it comes to board reviews. Since a college, university, or university system typically has only one governing board, there are no true "peers" to provide the lateral component. The only stakeholder group that remains consists of the faculty, staff, administration, and student body. And if single-point-of-view evaluation systems (such as appraisal only by one's direct supervisor) results in a limited and potentially biased view, the same problem occurs when an evaluation process contains only the "bottom-up" component.

Second, the vast majority of policies requiring evaluation of the governing board specify that the review must be a self-evaluation. But, as was seen earlier, self-evaluation is at best a highly imperfect process. Both individuals and groups who engage in self-evaluation regularly overemphasize their successes, downplay their weaknesses, and have no one other than themselves to hold them accountable for addressing the recommendations arising from the review. For this reason, self-evaluations tend to be formative in nature, even when a summative evaluation would be beneficial.

Third, a process that evaluates only the board as a whole, rather than the board's individual members, must remain a rather blunt instrument. Imagine, for example, an institution that didn't evaluate individual deans or department chairs but instead chose to evaluate only the council of deans or a department chairs advisory committee. No one would think that this very limited review process was at all adequate. And yet that's precisely the approach taken by most colleges and universities when it comes to reviewing its advisory board. In order for board reviews to be truly effective, evaluation of the group as a collective entity of the whole should be complemented by evaluation of the group's individual members.

Fourth, effective evaluation always begins with the question, "What are the assigned tasks, responsibilities, and goals of the person or body being evaluated?" Nevertheless, many board evaluation processes currently in place don't ask this question. Instead, they ask "Is the board effective?" without first defining what effectiveness actually means or "Did the board demonstrate good leadership?" without specifying the *type* of leadership most needed for an institutional governing board.

THE PURPOSE AND MISSION OF A GOVERNING BOARD

In order to overcome these challenges, board evaluations must be based on the group's stated purpose and mission. The Association of Governing Boards of Universities and Colleges (AGB) has identified eight primary responsibilities shared by most governing boards.

1. The board is responsible for determining the institution's mission.
2. Within the general practice of shared governance, the board establishes appropriate policies for the institution. (In other words, it established policies in the domain assigned to it without overstepping the bounds of responsibilities delegated to the faculty or administration.)
3. The board approves and is responsible for the institution's budget.
4. The board fosters open communication among the institution's various constituencies.
5. The board periodically reviews its policies to make sure that they remain efficient and appropriate to the institution's current needs.
6. The board appoints and assesses the performance of the institution's CEO.
7. The board clarifies the authority and responsibilities of other key administrators.
8. The board serves as a liaison between the institution and its community (Association of Governing Boards of Universities and Colleges, 2010, pp. 5–9).[1]

We might group these duties into several categories. Some, like determining the institution's mission, involve processes that occur only once or are repeated very rarely. Others, like reviewing the board's own policies, are typically done periodically, often on a three-year or five-year cycle. Still others, like approving and overseeing the budget, are done annually. And a final set of duties, like serving as a liaison between the institution and its community, involve actions that must be continually taken.

Therefore, by identifying the specific duties performed by the board during its current evaluation period, colleges and universities can develop a process that evaluates the most important responsibilities of the board at the moment. For example, if the current review period was one in which the board recruited and hired a new CEO, relevant issues for the evaluation might include the following.

- Did the board engage in a hiring process that was fair and equitable?
- Did the board make sufficient efforts to attract a diverse pool of applicants?
- Did the board make sufficient efforts to attract a highly competitive pool of applicants?
- Did the board screen applications objectively?
- Did the board take proper measures (in accordance with local laws) to preserve the confidentiality of applicants?
- Did the board hire a truly outstanding candidate?
- Did the board make efforts to provide the successful candidate with proper onboarding?

Similarly, for responsibilities that the board engages in continually, a well-designed evaluation process should review the extent to which those activities are being carried out effectively. Thus, in the case of serving as a liaison between the institution and its community, appropriate questions to ask would include the following.

- Did the board effectively bring the concerns of the community to the attention of the institution?
- Did the board effectively bring the concerns of the institution to the attention of the community?
- Did the board actively encourage participation in campus events by members of the community?
- Did the board actively encourage institutional outreach to the community by members of the faculty, staff, and student body?
- Did members of the board succeed in their role as ambassadors of the institution to the community?

When institutions specify the duties of their own governing boards—and best practices suggest that the institution's chart or bylaws *should* specify those duties—these lists of responsibilities can also provide a basis for the board's evaluation. For example, Dartmouth University specifies that its trustees have three primary responsibilities.

- Trustees must act as responsible fiduciaries through such activities as participating actively in the work of the board and its various committees, attending as many Dartmouth functions as feasible, and participating in self-evaluations and evaluations of board performance.
- They must advance the mission of Dartmouth by representing Dartmouth positively, serving the institution as a whole rather than the interests of any constituency, and contributing financially to the annual fund and capital campaigns at an appropriate level.
- They must also uphold the integrity of the board by maintaining confidentiality of all information proprietary to Dartmouth, speak for the board only when authorized to do so, refrain from requesting special considerations or favors, and avoiding conflicts of interest or the appearance thereof.

To further clarify how these responsibilities are to be carried out, the university notes that "The President reports to the Board as a whole, and the staff to the President" (Statement of Governance and Trustee Responsibilities, 2011).[2]

Similarly, the Revised Code of Washington (RCW 28B.50.140) specifies twenty-one responsibilities shared by community college boards within that state, including

- establishing, leasing, operating, equipping, and maintaining facilities;
- prescribing, with the assistance of the faculty, appropriate courses of study;
- hiring necessary employees to govern, manage, and operate residence halls; and
- delegating suitable powers to the presidents of institutions or districts (Washington State Legislature, 2018).[3]

Within this general framework, South Puget Sound Community College (SPSCC) clarifies that members of its board of trustees will have such responsibilities as

- establishing and maintaining institutional statements of mission, goals, and objectives.
- developing, in partnership with the college staff, long-range strategic plans.
- hiring and setting the salary of the college president.
- approving additional positions at the level of vice president.
- awarding or denying tenure to faculty members.
- dismissing or laying off faculty members.
- approving the college's annual budget.
- approving the initiation or the discontinuation of educational programs of study that lead to the award of a degree.
- and similar duties (Function, Purpose, and Authority of the Board of Trustees, 2017).[4]

If a college or university has a similar, well-articulated list of responsibilities for members of its governing board, that list can serve as an excellent stating point when developing a policy for evaluation of a governing board. For instance, imagine that an institution has assigned its board of regents responsibilities that combine those found at Dartmouth and SPSCC. An evaluation process for the regents of this hypothetical school might seek to determine whether members of the board have adequately done the following:

- participated actively in meetings of the board
- participated actively in meetings of the board's various committees
- participated actively in campus functions
- avoided conflicts of interest
- supported the annual fund
- supported capital projects
- maintained confidentiality of proprietary information

- refrained from requesting special considerations or favors
- developed a suitable strategic plan in partnership with the institution's faculty and administration
- approved the institution's annual budget
- engaged in similar duties that promote the mission of the institution

So, if your institution needs to develop or revise its board evaluation policies, you probably don't have to start from scratch. You can review the specific responsibilities set forth in your board's own charter or operating procedures to help answer the question, "What would success look like for this board?" But if it proves to be difficult to answer that question, the place for you to begin your development of a board evaluation process isn't with the process itself; it's with a clarification of the board's charter.

EVALUATING BOTH THE BOARD AND ITS MEMBERS

Nevertheless, even when basing an evaluation system for a school's governing board on the groups stated responsibilities, a problem can arise. For example, one of the duties mentioned in the section above was "participating actively in the work of the board." In evaluating whether this task has been performed, who is actually being evaluated? Is it the board as a whole or its individual members?

In the case of activities like attending and participating in board meetings, it's clear that it's the *members* of the board who are the focus of the evaluation, not the board itself. In fact, the responsibilities listed in the previous session can be divided into two groups. Some duties (such as establishing a mission statement, hiring the CEO, and approving the institution's annual budget) are clearly tasks performed by the board as a corporate entity. Others (such as contributing to the annual fund, attending campus events, and refraining from conflicts of interest) really only apply to the *members* of the board.

This distinction, while seemingly obvious, is glossed over in the vast majority of board evaluation processes. One reason why board evaluation processes aren't particularly effective, therefore, is that the job descriptions that institutions develop for their boards usually don't distinguish between what the board does and what individual members do. That blurring of these two categories can make it all but impossible for board reviews to help a college or university improve.

One institution that does do an excellent job of separating these two types of responsibilities is the Rochester Institute of Technology (RIT). In a statement titled *Board Responsibilities as a Corporate Body*, RIT declares this about its board:

1. Approves

    a. The assumptions, principles, and values which guide the University;
    b. The vision, mission, and strategic foci of the University;
    c. Broad policy affecting the entire University;
    d. The annual operating and capital budgets.

2. Assures

    a. The financial viability of the University;
    b. The fiduciary conduct of the University.

3. Evaluates the state of the University relevant to its vision and mission.
4. Appoints, supports, and evaluates the President.
5. Preserves the autonomy of the University and informs the community of its functions and accomplishments.
6. Assures that the Institute has an effective system of governance.
7. Provides for regular assessment of Board effectiveness.
8. Advises the University of forces external to the University that may have an influence on its mission, goals, and administrative policies.

9. Assumes responsibility (with administration support) for the ongoing education and development of Board members (Rochester Institute of Technology, n.d.)."[5]

At the same time, RIT clarifies that individual board members are expected to perform a far longer list of responsibilities. For example, each member of the board should do the following:

- To the extent of his or her ability, support RIT financially and assist it in acquiring support from other sources.
- Become sufficiently knowledgeable about the institution to make informed policy decisions.
- Participate in good faith decisions consistent with the school's mission.
- Have an excellent record of attendance at board meetings.
- Read all relevant material sent to board members and come to meetings prepared for active discussion of those items.
- Support majority decisions once they are made.
- Read, understand, and abide by the institution's policy on conflicts of interest.
- Become knowledgeable about any specific areas of RIT that relates to his or her committee assignments.
- Participate in the life of RIT by attending significant campus events, such as the start-of-the-academic-year convocation, commencement exercises, and other events where members can interact with representatives of the faculty, staff, and student body.
- Assist in advocating for legislation, government support, or other public assistance to benefit RIT.
- Provide sound advice and support to the president and administrative officers.
- Avoid interference in administrative matters.
- Follow normal channels of communication and decision making within the administration (Rochester Institute of Technology, n.d.).[6]

By making this type of distinction, the review process can be far more focused. Questions that are appropriate for the board as a whole (such as "During the evaluation period, did the board indeed evaluate the state of RIT relevant to its vision and mission?") don't become jumbled together with questions that really apply only to individual members (such as "Did Board Member X indeed support the majority decisions of the board once they were made?").

For this reason, if your school wishes to make its board evaluation process as effective as possible, it must first begin by making sure that the duties of the board are defined and then make sure that this list doesn't overlap with the expectations the school has for individual members of the board.

DEVELOPING A NEW APPROACH TO BOARD EVALUATIONS

If an institution were to develop a review process for its board based on this principle, what would it look like? In chapter 2, we encountered a fifteen-step process that avoids the difficulties commonly associated with review of administrators. If that approach is modified for use in board evaluations, it might look something like the following.

Step One

Identify the group that will oversee the evaluation process.

As we've seen, most policies on board evaluation require only a self-evaluation. But, if the review process is to be truly effective, it's important for other constituencies at the college or university to be consulted about the board's performance. Members of the board may understand what they were *trying* to do, but they may not always be aware of the full impact of their decisions on others. In order to expand the board's understanding of its effectiveness (or lack thereof), the evaluation process should begin with what was earlier called the *supervisory subcommittee* itself.

As with the subcommittee in charge of administrative review, the board's supervisory subcommittee should include representatives who are trained in econometrics, psychometrics, or other statistical methods commonly used in the social sciences. The process and instruments used to gather information should be vetted by the institution's IRB in order to ensure that they meet appropriate standards for data collection and adhere to the institution's policies on research involving human subjects. Doing so will help ensure that the process is fair and reliable and that the results are valid.

Other members of the supervisory subcommittee for a governing board might include board members from peer or aspirational institutions, representatives of the school's upper administration, middle management, faculty, and staff, and select representatives of other stakeholder groups regarded by the institution as most relevant to its traditions and missions. As was the case with administrative evaluations, a subcommittee of from eight to twelve people is large enough to include many different perspectives but small enough to make it easier for the team to schedule meetings and to achieve consensus.

Step Two

Have the subcommittee supervise the process of distinguishing board responsibilities from member responsibilities.

Because the responsibilities of the entire board and the responsibilities of individual members aren't the same, the supervising subcommittee should ask, "What does success look like for the board as a whole? What does success look like for a board member? And how do we design a process that evaluates both?"

The success of the board as a corporate body is important since the board, at most colleges and universities, occupies the highest rank in the institutional hierarchy. Evaluating the board is a key component in making sure that the school's mission statement and strategic plan are up to date, the president is held accountable for effective leadership, responsible fiscal policies are being followed, and day-to-day administration of the institution has been delegated to the right people.

Nevertheless, evaluating the board as a whole isn't enough. If you've ever served on a board, you're well aware that all too often most of the group's work is performed by only a small subset of members while other members merely go through the motions. As a result, it's important that there also be periodic review of each individual member to ensure that everyone is attending and actively participating in meetings, supporting the institution financially at an appropriate level, refraining from conflicts of interest and requests for special favors, representing the school favorably to the public, and engaging in other activities that advance the work of the board.

The supervisory subcommittee can thus establish separate but complementary processes that promote the best possible evaluation of everything the board and its members do. In most cases, evaluation of the board as a corporate entirety should occur annually. For evaluation of individual members, at the end of someone's first year, he or she should undergo a largely formative evaluation (with removal from the board possible, but only in the case of severe underperformance or misconduct), with a more thorough formative and summative evaluation every three years.

Step Three

Identify the specific behaviors or results that constitute success for both the board and its members.

While it's important to distinguish the responsibilities of the board as a whole from those of its members, an institution can't use that information alone to begin its review process. An effective evaluation process must also establish specific criteria for performance with regard to each of those responsibilities.

For example, it was suggested that one responsibility of the board as a corporate entity might be to ensure that the institution's strategic plan is up to date. What does that mean operationally? How will an unbiased reviewer determine what an up-to-date strategic plan looks like?

In a similar way, one suggested area of evaluation for individual board members was attendance at meetings. What, for this particular board, constitutes an *excellent* rate of attendance? What constitutes an *acceptable* rate of attendance? Until these criteria are set, it might be possible to say something like, "Ms. Regent attended two of the four plenary meetings of the governing board during the past year," without determining at all what that means in terms of whether Ms. Regent effectively performed her responsibilities.

In chapter 2, it was recommended that a template be created that would allow a reviewer to determine whether each performance objective was achieved. The same process can be used for board evaluations. For evaluations of the governing board, one possible template might be the following:

> During the evaluation period, the [board or member] will have demonstrated [general action phrase] by [achieving, completing, or reaching a specified numerical target in performing an observable activity].

Such a template could help define specific performance criteria like the following:

> During the evaluation period, the board will have demonstrated that the school's current strategic plan is up to date by reviewing the plan each September, discussing its progress with the school's administration each October or November, and voting either to ratify or to amend the plan no later than the spring plenary meeting.
>
> During the evaluation period, the member will have demonstrated adequate board attendance by active participation in at least 70 percent of plenary meetings, as well as all meetings of any committees or subcommittees on which the member serves.
>
> During the evaluation period, the board will have demonstrated appropriate fiduciary responsibility by approving the institution's an-

nual budget, reviewing and responding to the annual external audit, and overseeing expenditures on a quarterly basis.

During the evaluation period, the member will have demonstrated financial support of the institution by participating in the annual fund at the level agreed upon in the member's initial letter of appointment and pledging or facilitating the contribution of an additional amount as also stipulated in that initial letter of appointment.

Statements of criteria like these aren't yet ready to be included on evaluation forms to be completed by stakeholders since they're not phrased from the observer's perspective and are often what was referred to earlier as *double-barreled questions*. For example, the item about the board's fiduciary responsibilities conflates three different activities (four, if "reviewing and responding to the annual audit" are regarded as separate activities). But they do provide a concrete outline of the actions and behaviors that are expected from the board and its members.

Step Four

Rank the specific actions, behaviors, or results in order of priority for both the board and its members.

By this point in the process, the institution will have a list of observable—and, in many cases, measurable—activities that constitute the type of performance desirable from a governing board and its members. But that list is likely to be very long because governing boards have so many responsibilities. Though the school may initially wish to do so, it can't adequately evaluate all these activities, at least not in a single evaluation process. As should be clear by now, when an institution tries to evaluate too much, it ends up evaluating nothing at all.

The supervisory subcommittee's next goal should be to place these desirable actions, behaviors, and results, in a priority order. When it does so, it should once again be sure to separate what it intends to evaluate in the board as a whole from what it intends to evaluate in individual members. If, after doing so, each list still seems too long to order into a meaningful set of priorities, the subcommittee should use the *paired comparisons method of sorting* that was discussed in chapter 2. That method will both simplify the ranking process and help the subcommittee develop a more informative list than would result if it tried to reorder everything at once.

Step Five

Identify objective and reliable sources of information about those specific actions, behaviors, and results.

As was the case with administrators, governing boards and their members should conduct a self-evaluation as part of the review process. But, as was stated earlier, the problem with most board evaluation processes is that a self-evaluation is *all* that is done. Compounding this problem is the fact that, when board evaluations are mandated by legislatures or accrediting bodies, a self-evaluation is usually all that is *required*.

But like any group or individual, self-evaluation only tells you part of the story. Board members can't help but see their performance from their own perspective. And yet, that perspective may be limited or even untrustworthy when it comes to such matters as whether the board has avoided interference in administrative matters or whether its members have refrained from requesting special favors. The *administration* is in a much better position to know whether these particular goals have been met.

Similarly, members of the board shouldn't be the only ones evaluating whether they've interacted adequately with the faculty, staff, and student body. Those constituencies ought to be consulted as well. For this reason, the best possible evaluation of a board and its members should be some form of 360-degree evaluation.

For the board as a whole, insights can be gained by consulting members of other boards at peer or aspirational institutions who can comment on whether the board is well constituted, sufficiently diverse, active enough in the right areas of the institution's work (while simultaneously not interfering in areas best delegated to the administration and faculty), and generally adhering to the guidelines of groups like the Association of Governing Boards of Universities and Colleges, the American Council of Trustees and Alumni, and the Association of Community College Trustees. Parents of current students can comment on whether the needs and interests of their children are being adequately addressed by the board. The school's student government association can describe whether their relationship with the governing board is collegial, adversarial, or something else.

In the evaluation of individual board members, the board chair and the member's colleagues can discuss whether the member is an active participant in meetings, supportive of group decisions once they've been made, and willing to volunteer when committee assignments and other tasks must be completed. Members of the media can be surveyed about whether the member has acted as an effective ambassador of the institution.

For both the board as a whole and for individual members, members of the administration, faculty, staff, and student body can offer perspectives on whether their interests are being adequately considered, a positive image of the institution is being conveyed, and the institution has been well served throughout the current evaluation period.

Step Six

Assign a reasonable number of actions, behaviors, and results to each constituency for the purposes of gathering relevant information.

Recalling the earlier principle that the best evaluation forms contain between six and twelve items, you'll find it necessary to parcel out the areas of greatest concern for your evaluation among the constituencies you've identified as reliable sources of information. For the sake of making comparisons across stakeholder groups, two or three items might appear on all forms, with the remaining items addressing areas of special interest to that constituency.

For evaluation of the board as a corporate entity, questions that are asked of all respondents might deal with the board's accessibility, its effectiveness in advancing the institution's mission, and its diversity. For evaluation of individual board members, all constituencies might be asked about such activities as the degree to which the member has represented the institution favorably, attended important school events, or taken steps to become familiar with the needs and interests of that constituency.

It should come as no surprise that the number of respondents who declare themselves unable to judge the performance of the board or its members will be significantly higher for board evaluations it is for administrative evaluations. At most colleges and universities, the interaction of the board with individual professors, students, alumni, and parents is likely to be occasional at best. Even so, those constituencies need to be consulted since some of their representatives will have valuable experiences to share.

Even a few members of each constituency can be enough to provide important information about how the board and its members are perceived. But the supervising subcommittee must remember that perceptions aren't always the same thing as reality and that evaluation forms are only one data source among several that should be part of a thorough evaluation. (The subcommittee will certainly be aware of these considerations if it includes people with training in survey design and statistical analysis.)

Other sources might include progress in meeting the metrics set in the strategic plan, rates of financial contributions over time, records of attendance at plenary and committee meetings, and similar factors.

Step Seven

Communicate these criteria to all members of the board at the start of the evaluation period.

This step of the process once again parallels that of administrative evaluations. As with administrators, the set of criteria that will be used during an evaluation functions in much the same way that a grading rubric does in a college course: it helps the "grader" assess the performance of the person or group at the same time that it lets the person or group know what the expectations for performance are and which levels of performance will be considered acceptable. For this reason, once criteria have been established, they should always be communicated to the board and its members at the start of the evaluation process, not merely when the evaluation itself is about to be conducted.

Whenever possible, these criteria should include specific targets, and those targets should be scaled whenever appropriate. For example, a target requiring individual board members to contribute a minimum of $10,000 to the institution's annual fund is helpful but scaling the target will provide even better guidance. This type of scaling might look like the following. "A contribution of at least $5,000 to the annual fund will be regarded as the *minimum* required to meet the goal of ongoing institutional support. A contribution of at least $10,000 to the annual fund will be considered the *recommended* level of ongoing institutional support. A contribution of at least $20,000 to the annual fund will be considered an *excellent* level of ongoing institutional support."

Criteria that have been scaled in this way clarify for the board and its members what their goals for the year should be, and they make the performance appraisal far fairer and more systematic. Not every criteria established for board evaluation is quantifiable, of course, but at the very least they should always be phrased in such a way that it will be unambiguous to both the supervisory subcommittee and the board or board member whether the goal has been met.

Step Eight

Consult with additional experts from outside the institution to improve the process as well as the instruments that will be used for the evaluation.

No matter how much expertise was devoted to developing your board evaluation process and the forms used to gather information, it's always wise to receive the benefits of an external scan before the process gets under way. People with training in how performance reviews should be conducted may alert you to stakeholder groups that are over- or underrepresented in your process. Experts in survey design and analysis can point out ways in which instruments might be phrased or structured more efficiently.

Even though this type of external review is *always* desirable in evaluation processes, this step in the evaluation process can at times call for even greater diplomacy than usual when it is being conducted for review of the board or its members. After all, the board's own members may have designed the process and its forms. They may thus regard it as criticism of their own knowledge and skill when outside consultants recommend changes. It is not uncommon to hear complaints like, "I don't see what the problem is. This is exactly the way we do employee appraisals in my business, and we've never had an issue."

Appropriate representatives of the supervisory subcommittee may need, therefore, to explain the reasons why the types of evaluation that are suitable for one type of organizational culture are at times less than completely effective in a different organizational culture. For instance, what works in a hierarchical environment like a corporate structure may not be suitable in a highly collaborative structure like a governing board. Moreover, new research is being conducted continually on ways of improving evaluation processes, and research-focused institutions like colleges and universities should be at the forefront in trying out these newer approaches.

Step Nine

Gather and analyze information from appropriate stakeholder groups, including the members of the board itself.

Once the process has been externally reviewed and modified so that it takes full advantage of the suggestions made by the reviewers, the actual collection of data can begin. In most cases, the plan for how the evaluation will occur will be finalized weeks or even months before the actual collection of information is scheduled to begin. That's a good time for the supervisory subcommittee to proofread written documents, double check online forms to make sure that they work as intended and have systems in place for the automatic collection of routine information.

Routine information consists of objective pieces of data that don't have to be collected via evaluation forms. For example, the donations that a member or the entire board has contributed over the past year can be calculated directly from records kept in the office of advancement. Meeting attendance should also have been recorded in the group's minutes. If clear criteria have been established in these areas as described in Step Seven, it won't be necessary to ask stakeholders whether the performance of the board or board member has been adequate. The "score" will be sufficient to tell you that.

For example, if it's been established that a contribution of at least $20,000 to the annual fund will be considered an excellent level of ongoing institutional support, and the board member has contributed $35,000 over the past year, then it's obvious that the board member has met this target. Nothing would be gained by asking stakeholders, "In your view, did the board member provide a sufficient level of institutional support this year?"

Other areas of performance do require subjective judgments, however, and in these cases, perspectives will have to be solicited from appropriate stakeholder groups. After the information has been gathered, keep in mind while you are analyzing these data a fundamental principle that has been reiterated throughout this book: medians and modes are much more reliable measures of a constituency's "average" view than are arithmetic means. The latter can easily be distorted by one or two outlying values. So, even though most people are familiar with how means are calculated, it's best not to use them.

As with all performance reviews, self-evaluation should be an important part of this process. When reviewing individual board members, each person being reviewed should be given an opportunity to appraise his or her own performance. Seeing where there are substantial differences from the board member's self-evaluation and the views of other stakeholder groups can be much more informative than the scores themselves. In one example, learning that the school's administrators rate the board 4.1 on a 5-point scale in some area of performance tells you relatively little. But learning that the board rates itself only 1.3 while the administrators rate the board 4.1 tells you a great deal. It suggests that there is a large misperception between how well the board thinks it's doing and the progress that others are observing.

Step Ten

Have the subcommittee prepare its recommendations as to whether the performance of the board or board member meets the stated expectations.

In most of the evaluations conducted at a college or university, a supervisor such as a dean or department chair ultimately decides whether the person who is being evaluated has met expectations for the evaluation period. In the case of board evaluations, that's not possible since the board itself almost always occupies the highest rank in the institutional hierarchy. (Exceptions may occur at certain public institutions where a statewide office or commission outranks even the local governing board. In these cases, it is that higher ranking body that should render the final decision.)

Moreover, as we've seen, the policies of governing boards or the requirements of state legislatures often specify that the board must evaluate itself. How can an institution both meet those requirements and avoid the obvious limitations found when self-evaluation is the only type of evaluation that's conducted?

One solution is to have the supervisory subcommittee present its findings to the board in the form of recommendations, which must then be accepted, modified, or rejected by the board. While this system still makes it feasible for the governing board to ignore any criticism of its performance, it at least has the advantage of ensuring that the board has been *informed* of any weaknesses that constituencies have perceived and that the supervisory subcommittee is aware of any actions taken. Moreover, if a requirement were established that the subcommittee's recommendations be made public, it becomes much more difficult for a governing board simply to discount any criticism it doesn't like.

In the case of evaluations made of board *members*, the subcommittee's recommendations should be submitted to the board chair for further action. At certain institutions, a membership committee may also be asked to review the report of the subcommittee in order to maintain a consistently high level of performance among all members of the board. In either case, it would be the board's own policies that would hold members accountable for failures in meeting their commitments.

As was the case with administrative evaluations, the clearest way for performance to be "scored" in these recommendations is with a five-category ranking system (Greatly Exceeds Expectations, Exceeds Expectations, Meets Expectations, Fails to Meet Expectations, and Substantially Fails to Meet Expectations). In a formative evaluation, this approach helps clarify precisely where the accomplishments of the board or board member need to improve and the degree to which criteria either have or have not been met. In a summative evaluation, it helps avoid subjective adjustments such as, "The board hasn't achieved what we'd hoped for," or "This board member just isn't a good fit for us." Making clear judgments in this way is both fairer to the board and its members and more beneficial to the institution as a whole.

Step Eleven

Compare the results of the self-evaluation to the results provided by stakeholder groups.

As was seen in Step Nine, one of the most informative parts of an evaluation is not actually "scores" or "grades" assigned by any one constituency; it's the comparison between those "scores" or "grades" and what appears on the self-evaluation of the board or member. Sometimes those being evaluated are overly critical of their own performance. They blame themselves for not succeeding while other stakeholders give them credit for having made the effort.

More commonly, however, boards and their members are likely to judge themselves on the basis of their intentions, while others judge them on the basis of their results. In a well-designed evaluation process, both intentions and results matter. Leaders, particularly at the board level, sometimes have to take calculated risks, and not every risk will result in success. A self-evaluation can help put results into the proper context: "We may not have achieved our objective, but here's why we're better off because of what we attempted."

At the same time, results can't be ignored entirely. A governing board that never succeeds can't be regarded as effective no matter how noble its intentions were. Nor is it possible to ignore the perceptions of the faculty, staff, student body, and community. If a board is doing important work but regarded as unproductive by the school's stakeholders, it still has a problem. In this case, the problem lies in the area of communication. A significant issue may have gone unrecognized if the perceptions of constituent groups hadn't been compared to self-perceptions. And the difference between those two sets of perceptions will give the board an important direction to take as it enters the next evaluation cycle.

Step Twelve

Close the loop, part 1: Share the supervisory subcommittee's recommendations with the board or the member being evaluated.

Once the supervisory subcommittee has collected all of its information and developed recommendations about performance, the next step should be to share that information with the board. When the board is being evaluated as a corporate entity, those recommendations should be shared with the board as a whole unless the board's own policies state otherwise. When an individual is being evaluated, those recommendations should be shared with either the board chair or the membership committee. The chair or committee can then decide the appropriate actions to take next.

If demographic information has been collected, it's useful at this stage of the process to review whether there are any significant differences in responses from various stakeholder groups. For example,

- Do internal constituencies (such as the administration, faculty, and staff) have views at odds with those of external constituencies (such as parents, alumni, and members of the community)?
- Are there noticeable differences based on the gender of respondents?
- Do faculty members view the board or its members differently from administrators and/or staff members?
- Do members of minority groups have a view that is distinctly different from that of the majority population?

This type of demographic analysis helps provide a much more nuanced view of the board's performance than is possible by looking at aggregated results alone. That information takes on even greater significance when the board itself is more homogeneous than the stakeholders it serves.

Step Thirteen

Close the loop, part 2: Develop an action plan based on the formative advice contained in the subcommittee's recommendations.

In an administrative evaluation, it's possible that the process will end with a summative judgment that the administrator's term should end. In the evaluation of an individual board member, a similar result is possible. But, although technically feasible, it would be only in the rarest of cases that the subcommittee's recommendation would be that the board as a whole has so mishandled its duties that it should be replaced in toto. And even then, there is no guarantee that any board would accept such a recommendation.

As a result, the most common product to emerge from the evaluation of the board as a corporate entity will be formative advice. This advice is, in fact, one of the most compelling reasons for governing boards to move away from self-evaluation alone to something similar to a 360-degree evaluation. Just as an external scan may be useful in improving an evaluation process, so are the views of other constituencies useful when it comes to improving the board's performance.

After receiving the supervisory subcommittee's recommendations, therefore, the governing board should be encouraged to develop an action plan for addressing those recommendations. In some cases, that plan may consist of finding better ways to communicate genuine successes that were overlooked or misinterpreted by stakeholders. In other cases, the subcommittee's recommendations might serve as a "wake up call" that substantive change needs to occur. Either way, a primary goal of board evaluation will have been achieved: The board will have been alerted to concrete steps it can take in the future, and boards that truly care about their performance will take that advice seriously.

When individual members of the board are being evaluated, the chair or the membership committee can provide the formative advice from the subcommittee's report either formally (as a performance improvement plan that includes specific requirements and deadlines) or informally (as a mentor's guidance for personal growth). But this step should be taken seriously. It's almost impossible for the performance of the board as a whole to improve without improvements in the performance of individual members. In fact, the failure to evaluate individual members in even a review process that's solely formative can be a major reason why many board evaluations end up being little more than mere exercises that have only minimal lasting impact.

Step Fourteen

Close the loop, part 3: Inform other stakeholders of the evaluation's results to the extent that is appropriate.

Another useful strategy for ensuring that the board takes the evaluation process seriously is publicizing the subcommittee's findings to the greatest extent possible. If the recommendations are known only by the board, it becomes easier for the board to ignore them or at least to make them a low priority, but publicizing the subcommittee's recommendations helps "hold the board's feet to the fire." It encourages the board's constituents to ask what the members are doing about the report's conclusions and to follow up if they don't find the board's answers sufficient.

Nevertheless, in the case of evaluations involving individual members of the board, greater confidentiality will be required. These evaluations are in many ways similar to the administrative evaluations discussed in chapters 2 and 3. As "personnel matters"—even though the "personnel" here are not employees per se—the specific recommendations made by the subcommittee aren't suitable for widespread dissemination. Nevertheless, any summative *actions* taken by the board as a result of those recommendations should be a matter of public record.

As in the case of administrative evaluation, stakeholders who participated in the evaluation of individual board members should be notified that the process has concluded, assured that care was taken to preserve their confidentiality to the greatest extent possible, and informed whether the board member will be continued in his or her position. No other information should be shared.

Step Fifteen

Close the loop, part 4: Improve the process for next time.

Even the best evaluation process can always be improved. Each time the board or one of its members is evaluated, insights will emerge as to how the process can be enhanced for the future. Evaluation forms might be better phrased. Additional constituencies might be consulted. Greater efficiencies might be possible. Like the board itself, the board evaluation process should be expected to become better over time.

CONCLUSION

As with administrative evaluations, the fifteen steps of the board evaluation process can be divided into in three phases.

1. *Preparing for the evaluation:* Steps One through Eight.
2. *Conducting the evaluation:* Steps Nine through Eleven.
3. *Concluding the evaluation:* Steps Twelve through Fifteen.

Many of the steps in each phase serve as logical extensions of the previous phase. For example, identifying objective and reliable sources of information (Step Five) can be done almost simultaneously with identifying and ranking the specific behaviors or results relevant to the evaluation (Steps Three and Four). The reason for breaking the process down into fifteen discrete steps is to provide those involved in the process with something like a "preflight checklist" they can use to make sure that no important aspect of the process is overlooked. In actual practice, these steps flow organically from one another, and the entire procedure will be far less onerous than whatever is currently in place at most institutions.

KEY POINTS IN THIS CHAPTER

For ease of reference, the steps involved in effective evaluation of governing boards are summarized below in outline form.

A. Preparing for the evaluation

1. Identify the group that will oversee the evaluation process.
2. Have the subcommittee supervise the process of distinguishing board responsibilities from member responsibilities.
3. Identify the specific behaviors or results that constitute success for both the board and its members.
4. Rank the specific actions, behaviors, or results in order of priority for both the board and its members.

5. Identify objective and reliable sources of information about those specific actions, behaviors, and results.
6. Assign a reasonable number of actions, behaviors, and results to each constituency for the purposes of gathering relevant information.
7. Communicate these criteria to all members of the board at the start of the evaluation period.
8. Consult with additional experts from outside the institution to improve the process as well as the instruments that will be used for the evaluation.

B. Conducting the evaluation

9. Gather and analyze information from appropriate stakeholder groups, including the members of the board itself.
10. Have the subcommittee prepare its recommendations as to whether the performance of the board or board member meets the stated expectations.
11. Compare the results of the self-evaluation to the results provided by stakeholder groups.

C. Concluding the evaluation

12. Close the loop, part 1: Share the supervisory subcommittee's recommendations with the board or the member being evaluated.
13. Close the loop, part 2: Develop an action plan based on the formative advice contained in the subcommittee's recommendations.
14. Close the loop, part 3: Inform other stakeholders of the evaluation's results to the extent that is appropriate.
15. Close the loop, part 4: Improve the process for next time.

REFERENCES

Association of Governing Boards of Universities and Colleges. (2010). *Association of Governing Boards of Universities and Colleges'* statement on board responsibility for institutional governance. Washington, DC: Association of Governing Boards of Universities and Colleges.

Function, Purpose, and Authority of the Board of Trustees: South Puget Sound Community College. (2017). https://spscc.edu/policy/bord108.

Rochester Institute of Technology. (n.d.) Board of trustees. https://www.rit.edu/trustees#responsibilities.

Statement of Governance and Trustee Responsibilities: Dartmouth University. (2011). https://www.dartmouth.edu/~trustees/governance/statement.html.

Washington State Legislature. (2018). *RCW 28B.50.140: Boards of trustees—Powers and duties*. https://app.leg.wa.gov/RCW/default.aspx?cite=28B.50.140.

RESOURCES

Buller, J. L., & Reeves, D. M. (2018). *The five cultures of academic development: Crossing boundaries in higher education fundraising*. Washington, DC: CASE.

Chait, R. P. (1996). *Improving the performance of governing boards*. American Council on Education/Oryx Press Series on Higher Education. Phoenix, AZ: Oryx Press.

Oster, M. (2016). *Higher education board guidebook*. Chicago, IL: Grant Thornton. https://www.grantthornton.com/-/media/content-page-files/nfp/pdfs/2016/higher-ed-board-guide.ashx.

Schmidt, B. C. (2014). *Governance for a new era: A blueprint for higher education trustees*. Washington, DC: American Council of Trustees and Alumni. https://www.goacta.org/images/download/governance_for_a_new_era.pdf.

Scott, R. A. (2018). *How university boards work: A guide for trustees, officers, and leaders in higher education*. Baltimore, MD: Johns Hopkins University Press.

NOTES

1. The bullet points constitute a paraphrase, not a quotation.
2. With the exception of the passage in quotation marks, the section is a paraphrase, not a quote.
3. Again, a paraphrase, not a quotation.
4. Again, a paraphrase, not a quotation.
5. The nine bullet points are a quotation.
6. The bullet point list is a paraphrase and is abridged from a much longer list.

5

BEST PRACTICES IN BOARD EVALUATIONS

It can be even more difficult to revise how boards are evaluated than it is to change the process involved in administrative evaluation. While governing boards can be persuaded to adopt more stringent measures for measuring the effectiveness of presidents, provosts, and other senior administrators, they often seem less inclined to endorse a system that subjects themselves to greater scrutiny.

This challenge isn't limited to higher education. Corporate boards of directors also often resist having their own performance appraised rigorously. Even so, it's possible to find excellent examples both inside and outside of higher education where boards have taken steps to improve how they're evaluated. This chapter will explore those best practices as a way of illustrating that, even if boards are reluctant to adopt all the practices outlined in chapter 4, they may still follow the examples of others in developing a system that results in a candid, objective, and thorough assessment of their work.

BOARD EVALUATIONS IN THE CORPORATE WORLD

The first example to explore can be found in the corporate world. The Organisation for Economic Co-operation and Development (OECD) is an international group that works with governments and private citizens to address a broad array of social, economic, and environmental issues. In 2018, the OECD conducted a study in twenty different countries to identify what are regarded as best practices in the evaluation of corporate boards of directors around the world.

These were the questions the OECD was trying to answer:

- Are there any legal or regulatory requirements or practices that *require* a board (or its committees) to engage in board evaluation?
- Whether they are required or not, how frequently do evaluations take place?
- Who conducts the evaluations?
- At the end of the process, what do companies disclose regarding the results of their evaluations (OECD, 2018, p. 9)?[1]

As might be expected in any survey of nations that was diverse enough to include China as well as the United Kingdom, Israel as well as Turkey, and the United States as well as Singapore, more differences than similarities emerged during the course of the OECD's study. Nevertheless, the organization found several important commonalities that it identified as the four best practices to be followed in the evaluation of corporate boards.

1. *Frequency of evaluation.* Because of rapid changes in international marketplace, the OECD recommends that "boards of directors may need to conduct evaluations more than once a year or even continuously assess their performance through a process of constant evaluation. However, reporting of evaluation may only be necessary once a year" (OECD, 2018, p. 17).
2. *Subjects of evaluation.* In order to provide a thorough and meaningful appraisal, the OECD recommends that review processes should "include the board, its members (executive, non-executive and independent members) and board committees in the evaluation process" (OECD, 2018, p. 17). In its conclusion, the group reiterates that "[b]oard evaluation needs to be based on, and

include the assessment of, both the committees and individual board members" (OECD, 2018, p. 21). Self-evaluation of the board as a whole isn't enough.
3. *Supervision of evaluation.* As a way of providing a robust and credible evaluation, OECD recommends that "either the chair, lead independent director, [i.e., a specially elected non-employee member of the board], or board committee (usually the nominating committee), should be explicitly made responsible for the process. They should drive the process, involve the right people (including third party consultants, if necessary), and ensure that their colleague-directors are actively engaged" (OECD, 2018, p. 18; amplification within brackets is the author's). In order to clarify its point that "the right people" should be involved in the evaluation process, the OECD later emphasizes that "[t]he board member or committee driving the evaluation process should actively involve *external experts* if, and when, necessary" (OECD, 2018, p. 21; emphasis added). The OECD further recommends that information about the board's performance should be gathered from questionnaires that contain both multiple-choice and open-ended items, interviews with individual board members, and the company's own financial data.
4. *Dissemination of results.* In order to encourage the maximum amount of transparency, the OECD recommends that the results of the evaluation be reported, not only according to standards imposed by local law, but in a way that "enables investors and other stakeholders to review the process on a year-on-year basis and also makes it possible to keep track of improvements and issues" (OECD, 2018, p. 19). The group notes that this "disclosure should contain an action plan" for the future (OECD, 2018, p. 21).

Finally, the OECD concludes that board evaluation should not focus merely on the attainment of metrics in such areas as production and profit alone but should also "assess the composition and diversity of the board" (OECD, 2018, p. 21).

A similar list of best practices for board evaluation was independently developed by Geoffrey Kiel, emeritus professor in the School of Business at the University of Queensland, and James Beck, the managing director of Effective Governance, a privately owned advisory firm. Comparable results have emerged from studies conducted by the legal firm Gibson, Dunn & Crutcher and by Holly Gregory, a partner in the legal firm Sidley Austin (Gibson, Dunn, & Crutcher, 2016; Gregory, 2019; Kiel & Beck, 2018).

At this point, an objection might be made that simply because consultants and lawyers *suggested* that corporate boards follow these best practices, is there any evidence that companies have actually implemented them? As a matter of fact, there is, and the companies that have adopted international best practices in board evaluation have found the improvements to be invaluable. For example, the international technology company Shilp Gravures declares the following in its board evaluation policy.

> Behavioral psychologists and organizational learning experts agree that people and organisations cannot learn without feedback. No matter how good a Board is, it is bound to get better if it is reviewed intelligently. (Shilp Gravures Limited, 2019)[2]

In addition, among the numerous examples of corporations that have adopted the practices recommended above, leading examples include the following:

- The investment banking firm Goldman Sachs, requires that its board of directors be evaluated "at least annually," not only for the company's performance, but also for the effectiveness of its leadership structure and for the qualifications of its members in leadership positions (Goldman Sachs, 2019).
- The media conglomerate known as the Fox Corporation, which similarly requires that its board be evaluated "at least annually" and that all members of the board should complete a self-evaluation "that includes an assessment, among other things, of the

Board's maintenance and implementation of the Company's standards of conduct and corporate governance policies. The review shall seek to identify specific areas, if any, in need of improvement or strengthening and shall culminate in a discussion by the full Board of the results and any actions to be taken" (Fox Corporation, 2019).

- The information technology firm, Cisco, conducts annual evaluations, not only of the board itself, but also of each board committee and of each individual member. "The results of the performance evaluations are considered to improve the effectiveness of the Board, its committees, and its members, as appropriate" (Cisco, 2019, p. 3).
- The security depository firm known as Central Depository Services (India) conducts a thorough evaluation each year of the board as a corporate entity, each of the board's committees, and each member individually. The evaluation of independent board members is summative, with the result that "the Nomination and Remuneration Committee shall determine whether to extend or continue the term of appointment of each Independent Director, on the basis of the report of performance evaluation." Moreover, the evaluation process includes a formative element that results in the development of an action plan for improvement on any item for which the board, one of its committees, or one of its members receives an average score of 4.5 or less on a 5-point scale where 1 is the lowest score and 5 is the highest. Finally, "the manner in which the performance evaluation has been done by the Board of its own performance, performance of various Board Committees and individual Directors will be made [public] by the Board in the Board's report. Further, the Board's report containing such statement will be made available for the review of shareholders at the general meeting of the Company." Central Depository Services (India) even publishes the specific evaluation forms it uses in its process, several items from which will be adapted for the evalua-

tion form item list later in this chapter (Central Depository Services [India] Limited, 2019).

Similar policies at many other for-profit companies exist, but even this small sample should be enough to indicate to college and university governing boards that they can't argue against comprehensive annual evaluations of the full board, its committees, and each member because such reviews aren't feasible "in the real world." To the contrary, corporate boards—including many of the corporate boards on which their fellow members probably serve—conduct comprehensive evaluations all the time.

GASTON COLLEGE

Adoption of the best practices outlined above isn't limited to the corporate world. Institutions ranging from small community colleges to large research universities have adopted practices that can serve as models for other institutions. One such example is Gaston College, a multicampus community college located in North Carolina.

Gaston's board evaluation process is based primarily on four sets of criteria: the college's own statement on the board's roles and responsibilities and three documents provided by the Association of Community College Trustees Guide to Ethical Governance (ACCT):

- *Trusteeship in Community Colleges: A Guide for Effective Governance* (Smith, 2000)
- The *Guide to Ethical Governance* (Association of Community College Trustees, n.d.a)
- An item bank of over a hundred quantitative and open-ended questions for possible use on self-evaluation instruments (Association of Community College Trustees, n.d.b)

Although the ACCT itself says that "[b]oard self-evaluation instruments usually contain 30–40 items plus a few open-ended questions" (Association of Community College Trustees, n.d.b)—far too many items, as we've seen repeatedly, for truly informative evaluations because of the halo effect but useful as an indication of the school's commitment to thoroughness—Gaston focuses its review process on four key areas:

- Board roles and responsibilities
- Meetings and decision making
- The president's evaluation process and relations with other constituencies
- Board advocacy

The college also limits the number of open-ended questions on its evaluation form with the result that respondents are less likely to ignore those questions (Skinner, Watson, Smith, and Campbell, 2018).

Although the Gaston process is limited to self-evaluation and addresses only the board as a corporate entity, not its individual members, it does reflect several best practices:

- Each year the process itself is reviewed to determine if improvements are needed.
- Information is collected and tabulated electronically through an online survey site.
- The college's information technology staff then analyzes the aggregated responses before sending a report to the board chair.
- A board retreat is held for discussion of the formative results emerging from the self-evaluation (Skinner, Watson, Smith, & Campbell, 2018).[3]

The process is thus easy for respondents to complete, and the results are easy for the institution to compile. Use of an online survey protects the anonymity of those completing the instrument and avoids the possibility that paper forms may be lost or incorrectly tabulated.

COMMUNITY COLLEGE LEAGUE OF CALIFORNIA

In many ways, community colleges and their organizations like the ACCT and Gaston College are at the forefront in developing model board evaluation policies. Another group that offers institutions superb guidance in how these evaluations should be conducted is the Community College League of California (CCLC). In its guide titled *Assessing Board Effectiveness*, the CCLC states that the desired outcomes of a board self-evaluation include:

- a summary of what the board does well and its accomplishments;
- a better understanding of what is needed from each trustee and the CEO to be an effective board and board/CEO team;
- an assessment of progress on the prior year's goals and identify what needs to be completed; and
- goals and tasks for the coming year related to board performance and its leadership for district goals (Community College League of California, n.d., p. 3).[4]

Those goals are desirable for any college or university, and the CCLC outlines a practical roadmap on how to achieve them.

First, it notes that annual evaluations of the board's priorities and progress on achieving its goals should be supplemented by a far more comprehensive review process that is conducted every two or three years. Second, it recommends that surveys used to gather information be adapted to reflect local areas of concern rather than merely relying on generic evaluation instruments. Third, it suggests that quantitative information be combined with interviews of board members, which are preferably conducted by a well-trained and objective external consultant.

Among the other best practices discussed in the CCLC's guide are the following:

- All board members—not merely those who are experienced and who are not serving on the board ex officio—should be consulted

during the evaluation. New board members may see the board's operations with fresh eyes and identify concerns that long-standing members no longer observe. Student members may bring the perspective of one of the institution's most important stakeholder groups to issues about which board members are unaware.
- Community members and other constituent groups should also be consulted during the review process. Thus, even if the appraisal is called a self-evaluation, the board should not ignore how its actions appear to affect other stakeholders.
- The opinions of these stakeholder groups should, however, not be taken at face value. "Respondents may have expectations for the board that do not reflect appropriate roles and responsibilities. It is not unusual that trustees learn that college constituencies are unaware of governing board roles and responsibilities. A negative evaluation may result from board decisions that were unpopular with one or more internal constituencies, even though the board was acting for the good of the entire district or community" (Community College League of California, n.d., p. 7).
- An evaluation should include, not only a "snapshot" of the status quo, but also a plan for building on strengths and improving areas of weakness.

Like the ACCT, the CCLC also provides a bank of items for institutions to draw upon during their evaluation processes. Several suggestions from this item bank will be adapted for inclusion among the recommendations appearing later in this chapter.

NORTH CAROLINA STATE UNIVERSITY

North Carolina State University (NC State), located in Raleigh, began as a land-grant college in 1887 and is now a major research university that, along with the University of North Carolina at Chapel Hill and Duke University, serves as one of the three anchors forming the region's Research Triangle. As required by North Carolina's board of governors, NC State's governing board conducts a thorough self-evaluation every four years. The goal of this evaluation is to improve the effectiveness both of the board as a whole and of the individual members who constitute that board.

At the heart of its comprehensive process, NC State's board conducts a self-evaluation that is complemented by an effectiveness survey completed by select members of the chancellor's cabinet and other senior leaders. As an example of how the results of this process are used, after information was gathered in 2017, members of the board were presented with the results of their own self-appraisals alongside the results of the effectiveness survey taken by the school's administrators. By doing so, the board was able to highlight certain areas of general agreement (such as a perception that the general composition of the board and its committees is adequate but that the process for setting the agenda of meetings could be improved) and of disagreement (such as a belief among senior administrators, not shared by board members, that some of the trustees may have insufficient experience or expertise in the issues addressed by the board).

Quantitative information collected during the evaluation process revealed that members were highly successful in making personal financial commitments to the university (with over 90 percent of the members having made pledges or contributions) but less successful in keeping up with campus news publications or attending campus events during the past year (in each case, a full 62 percent hadn't done so).

These results, as well as other insights resulting from the board members' self-evaluation instrument and the administrators' effectiveness survey, were discussed by the board at a half-day meeting devoted entirely to appraising the group's performance. On the basis of this information, concrete action items were developed that were intended, upon implementation, to enhance each member's service to NC State and the overall success of the board.

Best practices seen in NC State's process include the following:

- There was meaningful use of insights provided by at least one stakeholder group (even though broader consultation would have been desirable) rather than reliance on self-assessment alone.
- Opinions that were collected through surveys were supplemented by quantitative data on such matters as level of financial support and campus involvement.
- Data was gathered through a secure, password-protected online system that provided automatic tabulation.
- The respondents' anonymity was safeguarded by presenting only aggregated data to the board. No personally identifying information such as email addresses or university ID numbers was connected to any data that were shared.
- Although the survey instruments were longer than recommended in this book, care was taken to ensure that no respondent would require more than ten minutes to complete his or her assigned survey.
- Multiple reminders were sent to participants in the survey to encourage the highest possible response rate.

(See NC State University Board of Trustees Self-Assessment, 2017.)

BEST PRACTICES IN DEVELOPING EVALUATION INSTRUMENTS

While many colleges and universities lag behind their peers in adopting best practices for board evaluation, there is one area in which many schools excel: creating significant questions for the evaluation instruments they create. In addition, many institutions either publicly disseminate these questions or post the item bank from their survey questions are selected.

Examples of institutions that have published their board valuation instruments include Dalhousie University in Canada (Dalhousie University, 2005), the Southern University and A&M College System in Louisiana (Southern University and A&M College System [2018]), and

North Carolina State University (NC State University Board of Trustees Self-Assessment, 2017). Outside of higher education, some for-profit companies, such as Central Depository Services (India) Limited (2019), also publish their board evaluation instruments.

By combining the best items that appear on these instruments with the most effective questions in the item banks created by the ACCT (Association of Community College Trustees, n.d.b) and the CCLC (Community College League of California, Appendix B), individual schools can draw from a wealth of resources when creating their own board evaluation forms.

A sample of how such an item bank might look appears below. But as with the similar item bank for administrative evaluations that appeared in chapter 3, it's important to note that what's presented here isn't intended to be used as an evaluation form itself. Instead, institutions should draw a few, select items from this list, focusing on questions that relate most closely to what is important to them and what can readily be observed by the stakeholder group completing the form.

Different items are appropriate for the evaluation of the board as a whole and for evaluation of the board's individual members. For this reason, the item bank in this chapter has been divided into two parts, with the first part intended for evaluation of the board as a corporate entity.

Board Organization

- The board has written policies that clarify its role in the governance of the institution.
- The board has written policies that clarify the limits of its powers.
- Board membership is appropriately diverse.
- The responsibilities assigned to officers of the board are clear.
- The board meets its responsibilities.
- The board follows a strong code of ethics.
- The board has an adequate number of standing committees.
- The board has the right combination of standing committees.

- The membership of the board's standing committees is suitably diverse.
- In matters other than diversity, the membership of the board's standing committees has the proper composition.
- The scope of the charge assigned to each committee is appropriate.
- The information flow from each standing committee to the full board is appropriate.
- The board provides sufficient opportunities for rotating membership within committees.
- The board provides sufficient opportunities for rotating leadership positions.

BOARD LOGISTICS

- The board regularly reviews the institution's mission statement.
- Board meetings allow enough time for suitable discussion.
- Board meetings are conducted efficiently.
- Board meetings are collegial.
- Meeting agendas are relevant to the work of the board.
- Meeting agendas clearly reflect the board's priorities.
- Materials distributed in advance of board meetings are adequate to permit the members to understand agenda items.
- Materials distributed at board meetings are adequate to permit the members to make informed decisions.
- Members have adequate input into the setting of meeting agendas.
- Adequate logistical support is available for conducting board meetings.
- The board periodically evaluates its policies.
- The minutes of board meetings accurately reflect the deliberations and decisions of the board.
- Dissenting views are recorded in the minutes of board meetings.

Board Actions

- Actions of the board are not subject to undue influence by a minority of its members.
- Actions of the board are not subject to undue influence by external forces.
- When the board reaches a collective decision, members support it even if they initially preferred another approach.
- The board makes decisions only after its members have explored alternative perspectives or approaches.
- In its discussions, the board focuses on policy, not on matters more appropriately assigned or delegated to the faculty, staff, or administration.
- When developing educational policies, the board appropriately seeks advice and recommendations from the faculty, staff, students, and administration.
- The board bases its decisions in terms of what is best for students.
- The board bases its decisions in terms of what is best for employees of the institution.
- The board has implemented a policy that provides employees with a grievance procedure.
- The board considers issues independently, not acting merely as a "rubber stamp" for the administration.
- The board expresses its authority only as a unit.

Board Development

- The board's recruitment and selection process for new members attracts excellent candidates.
- New members are properly trained in the operations of the board.
- Opportunities are provided for ongoing members to remain up to date in the effective operation of governing boards.
- Continuing members have adequate opportunities for training in the operations of this governing board.

BEST PRACTICES IN BOARD EVALUATIONS

- Board members have been informed that they have no legal authority outside of board meetings.

Selection and Supervision of Key Administrators

- The board has written policies that distinguish between its role (policy making) and the role of the CEO (administration).
- The job description for the CEO is up to date.
- In its most recent search, the board took steps to attract a pool of highly qualified candidates for the position of CEO.
- In its most recent search, the board took steps to attract a pool of suitably diverse candidates for the position of CEO.
- In its most recent search, the board hired an excellent CEO.
- The board works collaboratively with the CEO in setting his or her goals for the future.
- The board has an adequate process in place for the evaluation of the CEO.
- The board has recently conducted a thorough evaluation of the CEO.
- The board sets clear expectations for the CEO.
- The board has discussed with the CEO any concerns it has about his or her performance.
- The board regularly acknowledges the positive contributions of the CEO.
- The board consults with the CEO about the responsibilities assigned to key administrators.
- The board consults with the CEO about the selection of key administrators.
- The board supports the professional growth of the CEO.

Institutional Performance

- The board's actions have enhanced the institution.
- The board has identified the proper size of the institution in terms of student enrollment.

- The board has a plan in place for reaching the proper size of the institution in terms of student enrollment.
- The board has a plan in place for maintaining the proper size of the institution in terms of student enrollment.
- The board monitors the effectiveness of the institution's educational programs.
- The board requires the institution to conduct program reviews on a regular basis.
- The board regularly monitors the institution's progress on achieving its student learning outcomes.
- The board is appropriately involved in the accreditation process.
- The board benchmarks the institution's performance against peer institutions.
- The board benchmarks the institution's performance against the type of institutions that the school aspires to become.

Vision and Planning

- The board has an up-to-date strategic plan.
- The board uses scenario planning to evaluate strategic risks.
- The board adequately consults with the institution's CEO with regard to its plans for the future of the institution.
- The board adequately consults with the faculty with regard to its plans for the academic future of the institution.
- The board adequately consults with students with regard to their needs and interests.
- The board has approved an up-to-date facilities master plan.
- The board has approved an up-to-date policy on institutional safety and security.

Fiduciary Responsibility

- The board adheres to its fiduciary responsibility as outlined in its governance documents.

- The board is fully aware of the institution's fiscal condition.
- The board actively engages in budget planning.
- The board takes steps to ensure that the budget accurately reflects the institution's priorities.
- The board takes steps to ensure that the budget is well aligned with the institution's strategic plan.
- The board is appropriately involved in the supervision of the institution's investments.
- The board is appropriately involved in the supervision of the institution's management of its assets.
- The board has adopted policies for fiscal management that meet all applicable audit standards.
- The board works to secure adequate funding for the institution.

Campus Engagement

- The board has maintained a positive, constructive relationship with the CEO.
- The board has maintained positive, constructive relationships with key administrators other than the CEO.
- The board follows proper protocols regarding communication with the institution's employees.
- The board has maintained positive, constructive relationships with the faculty.
- The board has maintained positive, constructive relationships with students.
- Members of the board are regularly seen at campus events.
- Staff liaisons to the board communicate effectively with the members.

Community Engagement

- The board seeks community input when developing policies that affect the community at large.

- The board effectively represents the "voice" of the community.
- The board has strategies in place for involving the community in discussion of issues that affect it.
- The board has a policy for dealing with the media.

Open-Ended Items

- If you wish to explain your answer to any of the above items, please do so in the space below.
- Is there anything you wish we'd ask you but didn't? If so, please supply what you'd like to tell us in the space below.
- What, from your perspective, should be the single highest priority for the board during the coming year?

Demographic Information

Relationship to the institution

☐ Administrator
☐ Full-time faculty
☐ Part-time faculty
☐ Staff
☐ Student
☐ Community member
☐ Board member
☐ Other
☐ Prefer not to say

Gender

☐ Male
☐ Female
☐ Mixed gender, transitioning, exploring, or otherwise neither of the above
☐ Prefer not to say

Ethnicity

☐ White/Caucasian/European American
☐ Black/African/African American
☐ Latinx/Latino/Chicano/Hispanic
☐ Asian
☐ Native American/American Indian
☐ Multicultural/blended heritage
☐ Other
☐ Prefer not to say

How many years have you been associated with this institution? _____ year(s)

In processes where the respondent's relationship to the institution is already known—for example, surveys that are linked to specific email addresses or different colored forms that are distributed to different stakeholder groups—the section of the demographic information dealing with the respondent's institutional role may be omitted. Nevertheless, it's important to collect other types of demographic information because different groups may have distinctly different impressions of the board's effectiveness.

In any board evaluation process, impressions gained from inventories should always be combined with hard data that can be compiled by offices at the institution. For example, records of attendance at meetings, the percentage of the board contributing to fundraising initiatives, and the level of those contributions vis-à-vis the goals set for members should be provided directly from institutional records, allowing surveys to deal only with matters related directly to how the respondent perceives the board's effectiveness.

The second part of the item bank (below) is designed for evaluation of individual board members.

Mission and Vision

- The member is knowledgeable about the mission of the institution.
- The member avoids conflicts of interest with regard to the institution.
- The member avoids the *perception* of conflicts of interest with regard to the institution.
- The member maintains the confidentiality of privileged information.
- The member understands the legal obligations of serving on the board.
- The member demonstrates the highest level of integrity.
- The member demonstrates commitment to the mission of the institution.

Community Engagement

- The member has maintained good relationships with community leaders.
- The member is knowledgeable about community needs.
- The member is knowledgeable about community expectations.
- The member promotes the work of the institution in the community.

Knowledge and Development

- The member understands the mission of the institution.
- The member understands what is expected of board members.
- The member understands the institution's budget documents.
- The member understands the institution's financial audits and any recommendations resulting from them.
- During the past year, the member has actively engaged in training or development to remain up to date in how effective governing boards operate.
- The member studies issues adequately prior to board meetings.
- The member prepares adequately for board meetings.

- The member keeps apprised of current issues in higher education.
- The member demonstrates a clear understanding of how institutions of higher education operate.

Board Relations

- The member shows up for meetings on time.
- The member stays for the full duration of meetings.
- The member interacts respectfully with other board members.
- The member refrains from dominating meetings.
- The member is an *active* participant in meetings.
- The member is a *constructive* participant in meetings.
- Once a decision has been made, the member upholds the decision of the board.
- The member follows through on commitments made to the board.
- The member follows through on commitments made to the institution.

Institutional Relations

- The member has maintained a positive, constructive relationship with the CEO.
- The member has maintained positive, constructive relationships with key administrators other than the CEO.
- The member has maintained positive, constructive relationships with members of the faculty.
- The member has maintained positive, constructive relationships with members of the staff.
- The member has maintained positive, constructive relationships with students.
- The member has maintained positive, constructive relationships with alumni.
- The member is sensitive to the interests and concerns of the CEO.

- The member is sensitive to the interests and concerns of key administrators other than the CEO.
- The member is sensitive to the interests and concerns of the faculty.
- The member is sensitive to the interests and concerns of the students.
- The member is sensitive to the interests and concerns of the staff.
- The member is sensitive to the interests and concerns of alumni.
- The member refrains from attempting to manage employee work.

Open-Ended items

- If you wish to explain your answer to any of the above items, please do so in the space below.
- Is there anything you wish we'd ask you but didn't? If so, please supply what you'd like to tell us in the space below.

On the member's self-evaluation, it is highly recommended one additional open-ended item be included: Indicate the one area of your performance that you are most committed to improving in the future. It's also probably useful to include an opportunity for the member to indicate those areas in which he or she can best make a contribution to the board's work. That opportunity might look like the form that appears in figure 5.1.

On both inventories used in the evaluation of the board as a whole and those used in the evaluation of individual members, remember to base your selection of items on the following criterion: Which of the items would the particular stakeholder group completing the form have witnessed personally? Then phrase those items from the unique perspective of that constituency. For example, students are not useful sources for insight into whether the board's committees are suitably structured, but they may have important perspectives on the board's diversity. Faculty members may not be the best group to ask about the frequency of the board's meetings, but they can provide information

	I have special knowledge in these areas:	I have special interest in these areas:
Academic research	☐	☐
Budgeting	☐	☐
Event planning	☐	☐
Facilities management	☐	☐
Facilities planning	☐	☐
Faculty affairs	☐	☐
Fundraising	☐	☐
Government relations	☐	☐
Intercollegiate athletics	☐	☐
Investments	☐	☐
Leadership and management	☐	☐
Legal affairs	☐	☐
Marketing	☐	☐
Public relations	☐	☐
Real estate	☐	☐
Risk management	☐	☐
Strategic planning	☐	☐
Student affairs	☐	☐
Student recruitment	☐	☐

about whether a given member has been sensitive to their interests and concerns.

When reviewing the item banks above, some readers may object, "But we need to know about *all* these things." That objection certain has merit but, even so, remember that evaluation forms that try to assess too much end up assessing nothing at all. It's highly recommended, therefore, that each appraisal form address only a small number of the most important items so that those who complete the forms can give those items their full consideration.

CONCLUSION

Unless you're a member of a governing board, it can be far more challenging to modify the process of board evaluation than it can be to modify the process used to evaluate administrators. In many cases, the most that faculty, staff, and administrators can do is to suggest improvements to the board, making their case as compelling as possible so that the board will decide to follow those recommendations. But ultimately, unless there is a state law that mandates how evaluations are conducted, the procedure used for board evaluations is set by the board itself.

Nevertheless, the examples provided by Gaston College, the Association of Community College Trustees, the Community College League of California, and North Carolina State University prove that there are governing boards that are willing to adopt effective practices for evaluation because they understand the benefits those practices can produce. Educating members of the board about best practices in board evaluation within the context of higher education thus repays the effort it requires many times over.

KEY POINTS IN THIS CHAPTER

Of all the examples of best practices outlined in this chapter, the following should be considered the most important.

- Evaluation of the board as a corporate entity should always be complemented by evaluation of individual board members.
- Even in cases where the board is required to conduct a self-evaluation, that process should be overseen by a supervisory subcommittee that can make sure that existing policies are followed, ambitious standards are set, and objectivity is maintained.
- When a board is evaluated as a corporate entity, the results should be disseminated among appropriate stakeholder groups. When an individual board member is evaluated, the results should be re-

ported to the member, the board chair, and (where applicable) the membership committee.
- Board evaluation should focus, not merely on the attainment of growth metrics and learning outcomes, but they should also assess the diversity of the board and the expertise of its members.
- The board evaluation process should be reviewed annually to make sure that it's still meeting its objectives. If modifications seem desirable, they should be made before the next cycle of evaluations begins.
- A proper evaluation should include not only a summary of current strengths and weaknesses but also a plan for improvement.
- Evaluations should be based both on qualitative information gained from surveys/self-inventories and quantitative information obtained from records of attendance, levels of financial support, measurable outcomes, and similar sources.
- When information is collected electronically, care should be taken to protect the anonymity of the respondent as well as to verify that no respondent completes a survey more than once.
- Evaluation instruments should contain both quantifiable items and a few, carefully selected open-ended questions.

REFERENCES

Association of Community College Trustees (n.d.a). *Guide to ethical governance*. https://www.acct.org/page/guide-ethical-governance.

Association of Community College Trustees (n.d.b). *Board self-assessment instrument item bank*. https://www.mass.edu/foradmin/trustees/documents/Board%20Self-Assessment-%20Items%20from%20ACCT.pdf.

Central Depository Services (India) Limited. (2019). *Board evaluation policy*. https://www.cdslindia.com/downloads/IPO/Policy%20on%20Evaluation%20of%20the%20Board.pdf.

Cisco. (2019). *Corporate governance policies*. https://s2.q4cdn.com/951347115/files/doc_downloads/governance/2019/08/Corporate-Governance-Policies-August-2019.pdf.

Community College League of California. (n.d.). *Assessing board effectiveness: Resources for board of trustees self-evaluation*. https://files.eric.ed.gov/fulltext/ED509091.pdf.

Dalhousie University. (2005). *Board self-evaluation questionnaire*. https://library.wyo.gov/downloads/ldo/pdf/boards/BoardEval2.pdf.

Fox Corporation. (2019). *Statement of corporate governance*. https://www.foxcorporation.com/corporate-governance/statement-corporate-governance/.

Gibson, Dunn, & Crutcher, LLP. (2016). Board evaluations: Getting the most from the evaluation process. https://www.gibsondunn.com/wp-content/uploads/2016/05/Board-Evaluations-Getting-the-Most-from-the-Evaluation-Process.pdf.

Goldman Sachs (2019). *Corporate governance guidelines*. https://www.goldmansachs.com/investor-relations/corporate-governance/corporate-governance-documents/corp-gov-guidelines.pdf.

Gregory, H. J. (2019). *Board evaluation processes and related disclosures*. https://www.sidley.com/-/media/publications/plj_tb_aprmay19_governancecounselor.pdf.

Kiel, G., & Beck, J. (2018). *Board performance evaluations that add value*. https://corpgov.law.harvard.edu/2018/05/18/board-performance-evaluations-that-add-value/.

NC State University Board of Trustees Self-Assessment (2017). https://projects.ncsu.edu/project/botbook/public/2017/04/bot-tab11-self-assessment-public.pdf.

OECD. (2018). *Board evaluation: Overview of international practices*. https://www.oecd.org/daf/ca/Evaluating-Boards-of-Directors-2018.pdf.

Shilp Gravures Limited (2019). *Directors' performance evaluation policy*. https://www.shilpgravures.com/pdf/Directors%27%20Performance%20Evaluation%20Policy.pdf.

Skinner, P., Watson, J., Smith, J., & Campbell, S. (2018). *Board self-assessments and surveys*. http://ncacct.org/wp-content/uploads/2018/09/Surveys-Presentation.pdf.

Smith, C. J. (2000). *Trusteeship in community colleges: A guide for effective governance*. Washington, DC: Association of Community College Trustees.

Southern University and A&M College System. (2018). *Board self-evaluation policy*. http://sus.edu/assets/sus/SU_Board/Policies/SIGNED-Board-Self-Evaluation-Policy-and-Instrument-6-003-.pdf.

RESOURCES

Adams, R., Weisbach, M. S., & Hermalin, B. E. (2008). *The role of boards of directors in corporate governance: A conceptual framework and survey.* Cambridge, MA: National Bureau of Economic Research.

Krawiec, K. D., Conley, J. M., & Broome, L. L. (2013). The danger of difference: Tensions in directors' views of corporate board diversity. *University of Illinois Law Review*, 3, 919–58.

Missouri Department of Transportation. 2019. *Board self-evaluation policy*. https://www.mpers.org/wp-content/uploads/12-Board-Self-Evaluation-Policy-and-Criteria-Jan-2015.pdf.

Slesinger, L. H. (1996). *Self-assessment for nonprofit governing boards*. Washington, DC: National Center for Nonprofit Boards.

NOTES

1. The bullet points are a paraphrase, not a quote. Also note the British spelling of Organisation in the group's title.

2. The two different spellings (organizational/organisations) are in the original document.
3. All bullet lists in the section are paraphrases, not quotes.
4. The four subsequent bullet points form a single, continuous quote.

6

PUTTING IT ALL TOGETHER

Developing Synergy in Assessment, Program Review, Accreditation, and Evaluation

One of the leading concerns in efforts to improve the quality of higher education in recent years has been the principle of alignment. The idea behind strategic alignment is that the efforts of all the diverse departments, programs, and schools that constitute the modern college or university shouldn't be fragmented but rather should be coordinated so as to move together toward pursuit of a common goal.

Without alignment, it is argued, colleges and universities try to accomplish too much but end up accomplishing too little. The CEO's office develops one set of goals, the provost's office another, each dean and department chair still others, and the faculty yet others, with the result that the institution is pulled in many different directions at once. Diffusing effort in this way is ineffective, it is argued, and impedes progress.

When this type of alignment is discussed, the focus is usually on the institution's planning and pursuit of strategic objectives. Everything related to mission, vision, and goals needs to be aligned. The mission statement should inform the school's vision for the future, which should in turn shape the goals of the strategic plan, which should then direct the choices made by every program at the institution.

In actual practice, however, matters rarely flow that smoothly. The problem starts right at the beginning. As this author has argued in *Change Leadership in Higher Education* (2015), the vast majority of college or university mission statements are far too generic to inform a realistic vision for the future or provide much guidance for the strategic plan. Mission statements are drafted to appeal to everyone at once, reflecting the needs of both internal and external constituencies, and so they end up describing what *any* college or university does rather than describing the specific mission of that particular college or university (Buller, 2015, pp. 109–10, 116–19).

What needs to be done is for institutions to develop mission and vision statements, strategic plans, and annual goals that are truly distinctive and explain to stakeholders what the school does differently from its peers and how that difference makes it particularly suitable for certain students, researchers, donors, and other stakeholders. Alignment in this area has, regrettably, not lived up to its promise.

Nevertheless, there is another area in which institutions of higher education have a real opportunity to pursue alignment, and it is in this area that the evaluation of boards and administrators can play a significant role. As was noted in chapter 1, beginning in the 1960s and 1970s, colleges and universities increasingly developed an "accountability culture," an expectation that they document to the public whether they're actually doing the things they say they're doing.

Because of the accountability culture, learning outcomes are assessed in nearly every program, often in nearly every course. Entire programs are reviewed periodically for their quality, sustainability, and centrality to the institution's mission. And regional accreditation, which once occurred almost universally on a ten-year cycle, now often requires institutions to file reports more frequently.

This accountability culture has produced two camps at many institutions. On the one side, there are the "true believers" who are convinced that such processes as assessment, program review, and accreditation genuinely improve the quality of higher education and more than repay the time and resources they require.

On the other side, there are the skeptics who believe that the accountability culture, as it currently exists, simply increases the workload of faculty members and administrators without producing tangible benefits. These skeptics regard assessment and program review as little more than fads, distractions from teaching, and research developed by external groups that don't actually work in higher education and don't understand its culture.

Many of these skeptics extend their distrust to regional and specialized accreditation itself, regarding it as well intentioned originally but now little more than another bureaucracy they have to deal with. Under pressure from state and federal governments in the United States, the task of completing most accreditation processes has become so complex that, according to these skeptics, there is very little return on the investment of time and energy accreditation and reaccreditation require. Indeed, some claim that the current process of accreditation actually *lowers* the quality of higher education because it diverts faculty members from their primary responsibilities of teaching, research, and service.

You may not agree with the skeptics, but it's certainly possible to understand their frustration. A perception that higher education may not be worth its cost has led to calls for greater accountability. Greater accountability has led to the need for most schools to hire additional administrators and staff members to collect the data and file the reports demanded. These additional administrators and staff members have decreased the percentage of employees in higher education who are full-time teachers and researchers. So, there's a renewed perception that higher education may not be worth its cost, and the cycle continues.

But what if a different approach were taken? What if, instead of giving lip service to the alignment of mission statements, vision statements, strategic plans, and annual goals, efforts were made to align the accountability processes of assessment, program review, accreditation, and evaluation? In other words, what if all the efforts devoted to evaluation, assessment, program review, and accreditation weren't fragmented but rather coordinated toward pursuit of a common goal? Wouldn't such a change parallel other changes already occurring in higher education, such as the shift in focus from "inputs" (teaching, research, and service) to "outcomes" (learning, innovation, and impact)? Wouldn't that result be better than what exists now?

WHY SHOULD SYSTEMS OF ACCOUNTABILITY BE ALIGNED?

One objection is likely to be raised almost immediately. "But we've heard this all before," many (particularly those on the faculty) will argue. "What you're proposing is yet another management strategy that will take even more time away from our teaching and research. Our colleges and universities won't engage in the process you're proposing instead of all the efforts they're making in the areas of assessment, program review, and accreditation. They'll expect us to engage in this new process *in addition to* all these other administrative whims, merely increasing our workload without making the slightest improvement in educational quality."

This objection deserves to be taken seriously. As many faculty members and administrators have noted, higher education throughout its history has proven itself to be much more capable at addition than subtraction, developing new programs while failing to eliminate outdated ones, instituting additional policies and procedures without cutting back on existing red tape. And it's certainly true that the workload of faculty members and administrators has increased substantially as a result of higher education's accountability culture. The skeptics aren't wrong about that.

But there are several important reasons why schools can actually benefit from shifting more of their energy from planning to evaluation, from goals to results. First, as should surprise no one who has been actively involved in higher education for more than a few years, goal setting, particularly in the form of strategic planning, hasn't had a highly successful track record of improving teaching and research.

Too much planning occurs in higher education under the assumption that current needs and conditions will extend into the future. But that's a false assumption. Institutional needs change. The interests of students change. Laws change. The challenges facing society change. And so, even if institutions are successful in putting a long-term plan into place, the goals originally developed in that plan may no longer be relevant to the school's needs due to the passage of time.

Another problem with the way strategic planning is currently done in higher education is that legislators, administrators, and governing boards too often assume that bigger is better and that focusing on research creates a more prestigious institution than focusing on excellent teaching. Larger enrollment, the assumption goes, means that more tuition dollars will be available. Better research means that larger grants will be received.

But, as counterintuitive as it may seem, there isn't a straight-line correlation between higher enrollment and the availability of additional resources. Overstuffed classes can lead to declines in student performance, with the result that an initial gain in enrollment often produces a long-term decrease in enrollment. Students leave because their grades are too low for them to succeed or because they're looking for educational environments where they're not asked to share their classes with hundreds of other students.

Moreover, if schools take steps to reduce the number of those overstuffed classes by hiring more faculty members and building more classrooms, the net gain in increased tuition quickly turns into a net loss. Faculty members and new buildings are expensive. But the societal pressure to keep tuition as low as possible is immense. The trade-off may not be worth it for many colleges or universities.

Similarly, as more and more institutions pursue large research grants, the competition for those grants becomes increasingly fierce, requiring expanded investment in facilities, equipment, and research assistants. Making the matter worse is the fact that cuts in funding to many grants programs means that more and more schools are pursuing fewer and fewer grants even as they redirect faculty efforts in an attempt to become preeminent in research rather than teaching.

In order for strategic planning to be effective, therefore, it has to be supplemented by scenario planning (i.e., asking what our future might look like under various conditions that we ourselves can't control) and appreciative inquiry (i.e., asking how we can build on our existing strengths rather than try to become something we're not) But scenario planning and appreciative inquiry require effective evaluation as a prerequisite for planning. You can't get where you're going if you're not honest with yourself about where you are right now.

Second, shifting energy from planning to evaluation has the potential of increasing the buy-in of the stakeholder group most vital to the success of any college or university: the faculty. As it is now, many faculty members feel that boards and administrators claim credit when things go well but that professors take the blame when things go wrong. Faculty members feel that they're continually being evaluated through student ratings of instruction, annual reviews, merit increase appraisals, and the intense scrutiny they receive when they apply for promotion and tenure. Even though they're told that it's the curriculum that's examined through the process of assessment and organizational effectiveness that's examined through the process of program review, many faculty are left feeling that the focus is really on them. After all, it's their courses that are being assessed and their programs that are being reviewed.

Complicating this challenge is the tendency of some schools to do exactly what the cynics expect. They take information collected for *assessment* purposes (How well is this course or program doing?) and then use it for *evaluation* purposes (How well is the person offering this course or program doing?). For example, the grades assigned in courses, which should be a measure of *student* performance, sometimes are treated as a proxy for *faculty* performance. "If your students are performing poorly," college professors are asked, "doesn't that mean that you're teaching poorly?"

Nevertheless, even though the skeptics may dismiss them as fads, it has now become clear that assessment, program review, and student course evaluations are not going to go away anytime soon. But these processes can be made more palatable to the faculty by making it clear that college professors aren't the only employees of the institution who must undergo regular, rigorous evaluation. Setting the bar higher for administrators and governing boards, and then evaluating them to make sure that those standards are being met can be an important step in reducing skepticism.

Administrative and board evaluation sends the message that everyone at an institution, from entry-level students to the most senior members of the governing board, are regularly and objectively evaluated. This emphasis on evaluation occurs, not because the school is trying to punish underperformers, but because the school sees it as a vital part of its mission to help those who are not doing well become better and to help those who are good become great.

WHAT DOES EFFECTIVE ALIGNMENT OF EVALUATION LOOK LIKE?

Shifting an institution's focus from planning to evaluation doesn't mean that planning is eliminated. It simply means that a corrective occurs from placing far too great an emphasis on targets and metrics (even when those targets and metrics are trivial) to placing the right amount of emphasis on identifying current strengths and anticipating future challenges. The question most often asked of academic leaders today is, "Where is your institution headed?" Instead, it should be, "How is your institution helping its stakeholders and the world?" Aligning evaluation processes helps schools answer the second question.

To put it another way, planning should be subordinate to evaluation rather than having evaluation be subordinate to planning as it so often is now. That suggestion runs counter to what academic leaders have been told repeatedly for more than fifty years. "How," they're likely to ask,

"Can you evaluate progress if you don't first have a plan about where you're going?"

And yet that very question provides the answer that colleges and universities need: Setting goals and objectives should be merely one step in a process of continual institutional improvement. It shouldn't be the proverbial tail that wags the dog.

Here's the difference between what evaluation-oriented administration looks like and what currently exists. As it is now, academic leaders regard their primary function as developing plans for the future. Their implicit assumption is this: "We're not where we should be. We need to develop a roadmap to get somewhere else."

But that assumption begs a very important question: "Are we, in fact, not where we should be?" Unless you make that question the cornerstone of your entire process of improvement, you start making changes for the sake of change, even when preserving existing strengths would be a better option.

When you presume the need for change rather than inquire into the need for change, you're likely to assume that "moving up the higher education food chain" is synonymous with improvement. The result is that every community college feels it needs to become a four-year college, every four-year college feels it needs to become a university, every university to feel it needs to become a research university, and every research university to feel it needs to become a Research 1 university.

But even if progressing up that *cursus honorum* were possible for every school (which it isn't), the result would be to make higher education more homogeneous, not more richly diverse. The world would have a countless number of Research 1 universities, some of them excellent but many of them only satisfactory or worse, instead of a full range of excellent and diverse colleges and universities.

To be sure, the world does need excellent Research 1 universities. But it also needs excellent community colleges, four-year colleges, and teaching universities. So, the fundamental question every institution needs to ask is not "Where should we be going?" but "Who are we, and do our stakeholders still need the opportunities we provide?" If the opportunities provided by an institution are in fact no longer needed—if the school is in a death spiral of declining enrollments or is financially unsustainable for some other reason—then becoming a different type of institution would be warranted.

But if that's not the case, then planning change for the sake of change does a disservice to those constituencies that depend on the institution. Reaching that next rung on the institutional ladder sounds to students, parents, and donors something like the following: "Sure, we've built our reputation on excellent teaching. Students come here because of our excellent teaching. Donors contribute funding in order to support our excellent teaching. So, because that's what we're good at, we're not going to focus on it as much. Instead, we're going to emphasize instead something we've only been moderately successful at before: research." To many stakeholders, that doesn't sound like strategic planning; that sounds like betrayal.

Business theorists W. Chan Kim and Renée Mauborgne (2005) coined the terms *red ocean strategy* and *blue ocean strategy* to distinguish two ways in which corporations try to compete with one another. Red ocean strategy involves entering an existing market by introducing existing (though perhaps somewhat improved) products. The ocean is "red" because of all the "blood" spilled through the "feeding frenzy" caused by one company competing against another. To use a different metaphor, red ocean strategy assumes that the market is a pie; if I want to get a bigger piece, yours has to be smaller.

Blue ocean strategy, on the other hand, involves entering an uncontested market. Instead of defeating your competition, your goal is to make the competition irrelevant. If you want to earn money by taking people from place to place, you can try to create a better taxi service and compete with all other taxi companies using a red ocean strategy. Or you can do what Uber and Lyft did by inventing an entirely new way of taking people from place to place, thus making taxis irrelevant. The decline of the taxi industry and the increasing valuation of Uber and Lyft illustrate which strategy is winning—at least at the time this book is being written (Kim & Mauborgne, 2005).

Far too much strategic planning in higher education involves trying to move from a blue ocean environment where the school has already carved out its identity to a red ocean environment where the school is forced to compete with many other institutions that have established dominance in that market. For instance, these schools trade being a first-rate teaching college for being a second-rate research university. Contrary to their intentions, therefore, the school's preoccupation with planning has decreased their quality instead of improving it.

The solution is to avoid ignoring the question, "Who are we, and do our stakeholders still need the opportunities that we provide?" and instead to ask that question explicitly. If a planning focus assumes that there's a need for substantive change, an evaluation process determines whether there is even a need for such change. It isn't that colleges and universities shouldn't always try to become better (and admittedly becoming better does entail *some* sort of change) but rather that colleges and universities need to figure out whether they should get better at what they're already doing or whether they should be doing something else entirely.

Psychologists recognize that some people are never happy with their current situation in life but believe that they'll finally be happy if only they can reach "the next step"—whatever that step may be. This condition is known as *destination addiction*, and people who suffer from it are constantly striving for that next promotion, that next degree, that next romantic relationship, that next car/house/computer, or that next state or condition that they believe represents fulfillment. But soon after they reach this next step, they redefine happiness or success as the step beyond where they've just arrived and revert to being just as dissatisfied as they were before.

Colleges and universities frequently suffer from this type of destination addition, and the root cause of this condition can be traced directly to their fixation on planning. And yet, if evaluation is no longer regarded as a tool of planning but instead planning is regarded as a tool of evaluation, it's possible to break this cycle of continually striving to "reach the next level."

PUTTING IT ALL TOGETHER 153

Refocusing improvement on evaluation instead of planning requires schools to ask themselves the following questions.

1. *Who are we?* Knowing who you are as an institution results from exploring your school's distinctive role in higher education more completely than from simply adopting the vague generalities you'll probably find in your mission statement. It means taking a hard and critical look at what you actually do well, what you don't do as well as other colleges and universities, and how your history has brought you to your current point in your development.
2. *Whom do we serve?* Knowing your identity inevitably means knowing who your stakeholders are. What kinds of students do you attract? What kinds of students tend to persist until graduation? What are the needs of those students and how do you address those needs? Once you've answered these questions, move on to other constituencies served by your college or university. Even though most schools regard students as their single most important stakeholder group, they also need to look outward toward others who are affected by the decisions they make. Don Chu, the former dean of the School of Education at National University, distinguishes programs that are *closed systems* from programs that are *open systems*. A closed system only thinks internally. It regards its stakeholders solely as students, with perhaps the faculty, staff, and administration considered as an afterthought. An open system certainly sees itself as serving those constituencies but also recognizes the larger role it plays in society. It understands that the community, various professional groups and accrediting bodies, donors and potential donors, parents, governing and advisory boards, the media, and numerous others also constitute the school's stakeholders. Viewed from this perspective, the question you need to ask yourself becomes this: Out of all these groups, how well are we serving those that depend on us, and how is our mission and identity defined by the groups we serve? (Chu, 2012, 17–19).

3. *If we are effectively fulfilling our mission and serving our stakeholders, how can we do even better?* As we saw earlier, just because there's no need for radical or substantive change, that doesn't mean that institutions should remain static. Even a successful institution can benefit from reviewing its spending priorities from time to time in order to make certain that its budget is still aligned with its priorities. Small adjustments may be desirable in order to keep salaries, equipment, facilities, scholarships, and other resources at the level necessary for the school to remain successful.

4. *If we are not effectively fulfilling our mission, serving our stakeholders, or both, what are we going to do about it?* Candid self-assessment might indicate that there are institutional weaknesses that need to be addressed, outdated programs that need to be abandoned, or untapped possibilities that need to be explored. But the need for these changes, if it exists, ought to emerge from the process of evaluation, not simply presumed as inevitable. To be sure, some institutions will discover that they require substantive change because their mission is no longer relevant, their primary stakeholder groups have abandoned them, or they've been unsuccessful at meeting the needs of those stakeholder groups. *But those institutions will be in the minority.* Most colleges and universities will discover a few areas of weakness that they can improve through *core innovations* (i.e., making existing systems better) rather than *new growth innovations* (i.e., adopting entirely new systems). They will build on what they have not ignore what they have in order to become something new and different.

Approached in this way, all of a school's evaluation processes can be aligned under a single objective: How can the person, group, or program being evaluated perform its essential functions in the most effective way possible? Seeing all segments of the institution evaluated, faculty members will no longer feel that they're the only ones continually scrutinized for their performance. The accountability culture will give rise to a self-awareness culture.

With a renewed emphasis on evaluation, students, faculty members, staff members, administrators, governing boards, programs, and even entire offices or departments will all be held to the same high standard. All evaluation processes will be directed toward fulfilling a mission rather than measuring change for its own sake. The result will be a much better use of existing resources, and all of higher education will benefit.

WHERE CAN COLLEGES AND UNIVERSITIES GO FROM HERE?

Accomplishing this shift of emphasis will not be easy. Many people involved in higher education today are convinced that colleges and universities need radical change, not steady improvement, if they are going to flourish. But even though the process will be long, there are steps that faculty members and academic leaders can take right now in order to start aligning their evaluation systems.

In chapter 1, it was noted that, in the current accountability culture of higher education, everyone already seems to be evaluating everyone else. But the key phrase in that sentence is *seems to*. The evaluation processes that high-ranking administrators and board members currently undergo isn't nearly as comprehensive as that which students experience in pursuit of a degree or faculty members experience in pursuit of a promotion.

Administrators and governing boards must be persuaded that a superficial self-evaluation is never in the best interests of either themselves or the institutions they serve. The years of experience that colleges and universities have had with outcomes assessment, student and faculty evaluation processes, institutional review boards, and program reviews provide a roadmap for how administrators and governing boards can and should be evaluated. To fail to follow that roadmap would be tantamount to a dereliction of duties.

But it's not just at the institutional level that evaluation processes need to be improved. Accrediting bodies should also be encouraged to make their processes less cumbersome for institutions to accomplish. Accreditors are fond of saying that they do not represent some external agency that imposes rules on institutions, but that accrediting bodies consist solely of representatives from the institutions themselves. They support self-monitoring, not interfering with what colleges and universities do best. But that claim, while frequently heard, needs to be given much more than mere lip service. Institutions must reclaim the accreditation process for themselves, simplifying it so that they do not end up devoting to it the time and personnel so desperately needed elsewhere.

As it is now, most accreditation processes require institutions to make a compelling case that they are meeting a large set of standards and to provide reams of documentation in support of their claims. Off-site and/or on-site teams then review those materials and submit a recommendation to the voting members as to whether each standard is being met.

The process of gathering this documentation and writing the institution's case is so onerous that many institutions have resorted to perpetual reaccreditation review. They hire a full-time staff that does nothing else but compile and create the documentation required by the accreditors. They don't teach classes. They don't conduct research. They merely create accreditation documents.

That approach is both wasteful and ineffective. Assembling an accreditation application should require hours, not years. A far more effective approach would be for accreditation bodies to require institutions to provide the following:

1. A checklist of those items deemed absolutely essential for a college or university, such as a mission statement, a set of governance documents, conflict-of-interest policies for board members and employees, an assessment plan, procedures for the evaluation of programs and employees (including senior administrators and members off the governing board), and the like.

PUTTING IT ALL TOGETHER 157

2. A report of no more than ten pages describing one major strength that the institution has, accompanied by a plan explaining how success in that area will be increased even further over the next five years.
3. A report of no more than ten pages describing one major institutional weakness, accompanied by a plan for dealing with that weakness over the next five years.
4. One or two pages of data illustrating whether the two plans included in the institution's last five-year accreditation report were successful.

Under this system, it would not be the institution's responsibility to argue that its mission statement, set of governance documents, and the like were adequate, but the job of the accrediting body's offsite and/or on-site review teams to do so. As aligned with all the other evaluation approaches at the institution, the accreditors' report could include summative judgments (i.e., "This essential item is missing" or "This policy must be completely rewritten because . . ."), but would always include formative recommendations ("One way of making this policy even better would be to . . .").

For example, if an accrediting body didn't feel that the school's mission statement was sufficiently distinctive, it should say so and offer suggestions for improvement. If the group believed that the school's assessment plan or its implementation were deficient in some way, it should say so and offer suggestions for improvement. And if the accreditor concluded that administrators or board members were not being evaluated effectively, it should say so and offer suggestions for improvement.

In this way, outcomes assessment, program review, personnel evaluation, and accreditation wouldn't all be independent processes that compete with the time an institution can spend on teaching or research; they would be aligned processes all directed toward making the institution even better than it already is.

The irony of how higher education currently operates is that, although it functions within the context of an accountability culture, its current practice of accountability is solely directed toward change, growth, and innovation. As a result, change becomes rewarded even if it doesn't bring about improvement. But by refocusing the existing accountability culture on effectiveness and service to stakeholders, higher education will experience far less change for the sake of change and far more significant and ongoing improvement.

CONCLUSION

Some readers are likely to object that the recommendations made in this chapter are too minor. ("You're simply telling us to do many of the things we're already doing. All you're saying is that we should shift our focus slightly from setting goals to evaluating results.") At the same time, other readers might object that the recommendations above are too radical. ("You're trying to turn back the tide of fifty years or more on strategic planning and accreditation practices just to evaluate administrators and boards a bit better.")

The truth, as is so often the case, lies somewhere between these two extreme views. Colleges and universities today aren't, with a few notable exceptions, evaluating their administrators and governing boards as effectively as they should. Accrediting requirements are too cumbersome, forcing institutions to expend resources that could better be directed elsewhere. And too many institutions are neglecting ways in which they can improve by regarding growth and change as their primary objectives, not effectiveness in fulfilling their stated missions.

But the solution to these problems doesn't require a complete overhaul of the entire system of higher education. It certainly doesn't require the paradoxical recommendation that schools change even more in order to reduce their current overemphasis on change. It simply requires an adjustment of priorities from asking the question, "Where should we be going next?" to asking the questions, "Where are we now, and are we in the right place for the constituents we serve?"

This study began with the observation that new approaches to board and administrative evaluations have to be considered because many accrediting bodies are now requiring these evaluations. Ironically making administrative and board evaluations as effective as possible may well entail reforming those very accrediting bodies that require them. They, too, may discover that the questions, "Are we doing what we say we're doing in the most effective way possible and, if not, what are we going to do about it?" will lead them to answers that are unsettling and that require them to act differently.

KEY POINTS IN THIS CHAPTER

- Strategic alignment in higher education has traditionally been focused on coordinating an institution's mission, vision, strategic plan, and annual goals.
- But this type of alignment has rarely been successful because many institutional mission statements are overly generic and strategic plans are often about getting bigger and "moving up the higher education food chain" rather than building on existing strengths and improving services to stakeholders.
- A more effective type of alignment would be to coordinate the efforts made in such areas as evaluation, assessment, program review, and accreditation.
- Strategic planning has not lived up to its promise of improving the quality of teaching and research at many institutions.
- Accreditation processes should be part of an overall evaluation approach and made less onerous so that they do not divert time and energy from an institution's primary missions of teaching, research, and service.

REFERENCES

Buller, J. L. (2015). *Change leadership in higher education: A practical guide to academic transformation*. San Francisco, CA: Jossey-Bass.

Chu, D. (2012). *The department chair primer: What chairs need to know and do to make a difference*. San Francisco, CA: Jossey-Bass.

Kim, W. C., & Mauborgne, R. (2005). *Blue ocean strategy: How to create uncontested market space and make the competition irrelevant.* Boston, MA: Harvard Business Review Press.

RESOURCES

Carey, K., & Schneider, M. (2010). *Accountability in American higher education.* New York, NY: Palgrave Macmillan.

Gaston, P. L. (2014). *Higher education accreditation: How it's changing, why it must.* Sterling, VA: Stylus.

Kelchen, R. (2018). *Higher education accountability.* Baltimore, MD: Johns Hopkins University Press.

Lovell, C., Larson, T. E., Dean, D. R., & Longanecker, D. (2010). *Public policy and higher education.* (2nd ed.) New York: Learning Solutions.

Suskie, L. A., & Ikenberry, S. O. (2015). *Five dimensions of quality: A common sense guide to accreditation and accountability.* San Francisco, CA: Jossey-Bass.

OTHER BOOKS BY JEFFREY L. BULLER

- *Confronting Today's Issues: Opportunities and Challenges for School Administrators* (with Chad Prosser and Denise Spirou)
- *A Handbook for College and University Advisory Boards* (with Dianne M. Reeves)
- *Mindful Leadership: An Insight-Based Approach to College Administration*
- *Managing Time and Stress: A Guide for Academic Leaders to Accomplish What Matters*
- *Authentic Academic Leadership: A Values-Based Approach to College Administration*
- *The Five Cultures of Academic Development: Crossing Boundaries in Higher Education Fundraising* (with Dianne M. Reeves)
- *Hire the Right Faculty Member Every Time: Best Practices in Recruiting, Selecting, and Onboarding College Professors*
- *Best Practices for Faculty Search Committees: How to Review Applications and Interview Candidates*
- *Going for the Gold: How to Become a World-Class Academic Fundraiser* (with Dianne M. Reeves)
- *World-Class Fundraising Isn't a Solo Sport: The Team Approach to Academic Fundraising* (with Dianne M. Reeves)
- *A Toolkit for College Professors* (with Robert E. Cipriano)
- *A Toolkit for Department Chairs* (with Robert E. Cipriano)

OTHER BOOKS BY JEFFREY L. BULLER

- *Building Leadership Capacity: A Guide to Best Practices* (with Walter H. Gmelch)
- *Change Leadership in Higher Education: A Practical Guide to Academic Transformation*
- *Positive Academic Leadership: How to Stop Putting Out Fires and Start Making a Difference*
- *Best Practices in Faculty Evaluation: A Practical Guide for Academic Leaders*
- *Academic Leadership Day By Day: Small Steps That Lead to Great Success*
- *The Essential Department Chair: A Comprehensive Desk Reference*, Second Edition
- *The Essential Academic Dean: A Comprehensive Desk Reference*, Second Edition
- *The Essential College Professor: A Practical Guide to an Academic Career*

MORE ABOUT ATLAS

ATLAS: Academic Training, Leadership, & Assessment Services offers training programs, books, and materials dealing with collegiality and positive academic leadership. Its more than fifty highly interactive programs include the following:

- Introduction to Academic Leadership
- Team Building for Academic Leaders
- Time Management for Academic Leaders
- Stress Management for Academic Leaders
- Budgeting for Academic Leaders
- Decision Making for Academic Leaders
- Problem Solving for Academic Leaders
- Conflict Management for Academic Leaders
- Emotional Intelligence for Academic Leaders
- Effective Communication for Academic Leaders
- Work-Life Balance for Academic Leaders
- Best Practices in Academic Fundraising
- Protecting Yourself from a Toxic Work Environment

- Developing Leadership Capacity: How You Can Create a Leadership Development Program at Your Institution
- We've Got to Stop Meeting Like This: Leading Meetings Effectively
- Why Academic Leaders Must Lead Differently: Understanding the Organizational Culture of Higher Education
- Getting Organized: Taking Control of Your Schedule, Workspace, and Habits to Get More Done in Less Time with Lower Stress
- Collegiality and Teambuilding
- Change Leadership in Higher Education
- Promoting Faculty and Staff Engagement
- Best Practices in Faculty Recruitment and Hiring
- Best Practices in Faculty Evaluation
- Best Practices in Coaching and Mentoring
- Moving Forward: Training and Development for Advisory Boards
- Training the Trainers: How to Give Presentations and Provide Training the ATLAS Way
- Managing Up for Academic Leaders: How to Flourish When Dealing with Your Boss and Your Boss's Boss
- Creating a Culture of Student Success
- Positive Academic Leadership: How to Stop Putting Out Fires and Start Making a Difference
- Authentic Academic Leadership: A Values-Based Approach to Academic Leadership
- Mindful Academic Leadership: A Mindfulness-Based Approach to Academic Leadership
- Fostering a College University: An In-Depth Exploration of Collegiality in Higher Education
- Managing Conflict: An In-Depth Exploration of Conflict Management in Higher Education
- A Toolkit for College Professors
- A Toolkit for Department Chairs
- Exploring Academic Leadership: Is College/University Administration Right for Me?

ATLAS offers programs in half-day, full-day, and multiday formats. ATLAS also offers reduced prices on leadership books and sells materials that can be used to assess your institution or program:

- the Collegiality Assessment Matrix (CAM), which allows academic programs to evaluate the collegiality and civility of their faculty members in a consistent, objective, and reliable manner
- the Self-Assessment Matrix (S-AM), which is a self-evaluation version of the CAM
- the ATLAS Campus Climate and Moral Survey
- the ATLAS Faculty and Staff Engagement Survey

These assessment instruments are available in both electronic and paper formats. In addition, the ATLAS E-Newsletter addresses a variety of issues related to academic leadership and is sent free to subscribers.

For more information, contact:
ATLAS: Academic Training, Leadership, & Assessment Services
9154 Wooden Road
Raleigh, NC 27617
800-355-6742
www.atlasleadership.com
Email: questions@atlasleadership.com

INDEX

AAUP (American Association of University Professors), 62–64
ACCJC (Accrediting Commission for Community and Junior Colleges of the Western Association of Schools and Colleges), 4, 85
accountability: accountability culture, 144–145; historical perspective, 1–2; improving instruments of evaluation, 21–26; improving process of evaluation, 15–21; key points, 27–28; mandates, 3–6, 61, 138; performance reviews, 7–10; problems with evaluations, 6–15. *See also* evaluations of administrators; evaluations of governing boards; strategic alignment
accreditation process, 145, 156–158
Accrediting Commission for Community and Junior Colleges of the Western Association of Schools and Colleges (ACCJC), 4, 85
ACCT (Association of Community College Trustees), 73–74, 99, 120
actionable items on evaluation forms, 12
administration survey topics, 77–78
administrators: differing duties, 36; job descriptions, 34, 35–36; problems with evaluation process, 10–11; strategic objectives, 34; tactics and practices, 34. *See also* best practices in administrative evaluations; chief executive officers (CEOs); evaluations of administrators; steps in administrative evaluations; survey topics in administrative evaluations
Adobe (company), 7–8, 15–16
AGB (Association of Governing Boards of Universities and Colleges), 86–87, 99
ambiguity on evaluation forms, 12
American Association of University Professors (AAUP), 62–64
American Council of Trustees and Alumni, 99
arithmetic means as average score, 24–25, 51
Arreola, Raoul, 37–39
Assessing Board Effectiveness (CCLC), 122–123
AssessTEAM, 22
Association of Community College Trustees (ACCT), 73–74, 99, 120
Association of Governing Boards of Universities and Colleges (AGB), 86–87, 99

Beck, James, 118
best practices in administrative evaluations: from American Association of University Professors, 62–64; from Georgia College and State University, 64–66; instruments for, 73–74; key points, 82–83; not

reinventing, 81; from Southeastern Louisiana University, 68–70; from State University of New York, 66–68; from Texas Women's University, 70–72. *See also* survey topics in administrative evaluations
best practices in board evaluations: challenges of, 115; from Community College League of California, 122–123; from corporate world, 115–120; from Gaston College, 120–121; instruments for, 125–126; key points, 138–139; from North Carolina State University, 123–125
bias: reducing, 17–18; against women and other groups, 9–10, 14
blue ocean strategy, 151–152
boards. *See* governing boards
budgeting survey topics, 76–77
Buller, Jeffrey, 161–162

Carli, Linda, 14
Cecchi-Dimeglio, Paola, 17–18
Central Depository Services (India), 119
Change Leadership in Higher Education (Buller), 144
Check In Process of evaluation, 15–16
chief executive officers (CEOs): Board's role in hiring, 87–88; evaluation of, 5–6; job descriptions for, 35–36; potential problems with evaluating, 6–7. *See also* administrators
Chu, Don, 153
Cisco, 119
closed systems, 153
coach, leader as, 16–17
coaching tone in evaluation meetings, 54–55
communication survey topics, 75–76
Community College League of California (CCLC), 122–123
composite scores, 25
compound items on evaluation forms, 11, 74
comprehensive end-of-term reviews, 63
Conboy, Katie, 2
confidentiality, 63, 110
corporate boards, 115–120

crowdsourcing for performance data, 18, 50
Culture Amp, 22

Dartmouth University, 88–89
data collection and analysis. *See* information collection and analysis
demographic information about respondents, 50–51, 78–80, 108
destination addiction, 152
dissemination of evaluation results, 117
double-barreled questions, 11, 98

Eagley, Alice, 14
Eastern Kentucky University, 8
enrollment increases, 147
evaluation instruments. *See* instruments for rating performance
evaluation scales, 51–52
evaluations of administrators: concluding, 53–56, 57, 59; conducting, 50–53, 57, 58–59; importance of, 27, 149; improving, 15–21, 56; key points, 58–59; mandates and, 61; preparing for, 39–49, 57, 58; reasons for, 33–34, 64, 68. *See also* accountability; best practices in administrative evaluations; steps in administrative evaluations; survey topics in administrative evaluations; 360-degree evaluations
evaluations of governing boards: challenges of, 85–86; concluding, 107–110, 111, 112; conducting, 103–107, 111, 112; dual evaluations of board and individual members, 86, 91–94, 95–96; hypothetical process, 90–91; importance of, 27, 149; improving, 15–21, 110; preparing for, 94–103, 111, 111–112; templates for, 97–98. *See also* accountability; best practices in board evaluations; steps in board evaluations; survey topics in individual board member evaluations; survey topics in whole board evaluations; 360-degree evaluations
external evaluation forms, 49

faculty, evaluations of, 8–9, 37–39

INDEX

faculty role in administrative evaluations, 62–64, 65, 66–68, 69, 70–71
15Five (company), 16–17, 18
formative evaluations, 17, 54–55, 56, 70, 86, 109
Fox Corporation, 118
frequency of evaluations, 15, 16, 17; for administrators, 35, 62, 65, 67, 72; for boards, 96, 123; communicating expectations and, 47–48; for corporate entities, 116

Gaston College, 120–121
Georgia College and State University (GCSU), 64–66
Gibson, Dunn & Crutcher, 118
Goldman Sachs, 118
governing boards: CEOs and, 5–6, 6–7, 35–36, 45, 46; duties of, 86–91, 96–97; performance review process, 10–11; purpose and mission, 86–91; self-evaluation mandate, 3–5. *See also* best practices in board evaluations; evaluations of governing boards; steps in board evaluations; survey topics in individual board member evaluations; survey topics in whole board evaluations
grading rubrics, 47–48, 101–102
grants programs, 147
Grapevine, 22
Gregory, Holly, 118

halo effect, 11, 13, 73
Hassell, David, 16–17
Higgerson, Mary Lou, 19–21
How can we do better? question, 154

Ibarra, Herminia, 14
IDEA (vendor), 22
inconsistency of rating levels, 13
individual board members, 87, 97, 100, 101. *See also* governing boards; survey topics in individual board member evaluations
information collection and analysis: for administrative evaluations, 45–46, 50–51; for board evaluations, 100–101, 103–104; crowdsourcing for performance data, 18, 50; improving, 18–21
institutional environment survey topics, 76
institutional goals. *See* strategic alignment
institutional review board (IRB) approval process, 11, 18, 22, 40, 95
instruments for rating performance: best practices, 73–74, 125–126; effectiveness survey with self-evaluation, 124; elements of, 50; improving, 21–26; length of, 74; locally developed, 11–14; problems with, 11–14; standardized with customized, 67. *See also* self-evaluation; survey topics in administrative evaluations
interim administrative positions, 72
IRB (institutional review board) approval process, 11, 18, 22, 40, 95

job descriptions, 34, 35–36, 40–41, 57
Juvenal, 3

Kansas State University, 8
Kiel, Geoffrey, 118
Kim, W. Chan, 151–152

leadership survey items, 75
learning environment survey items, 76
length of evaluations, 13
letters in portfolios, 21
liaison role of boards, 88
Likert, Rensis, 13
Likert scale, 13, 23, 39
locally-developed evaluation instruments, 11–14

mandates, 3–6, 61, 138
Martin, Jonathan, 9
Martin, Kristina, 9
Mauborgne, Renée, 151–152
median as average score, 24–25, 51
mentoring and evaluation survey topics, 78
"middle managers" evaluation, 2
Midland College, 9
mission and vision statements, 143–145
mode as average score, 24–25, 51
Mosely, Eric, 18

multiple-choice items on evaluation forms, 12

National University, 153
NC State (North Carolina State University), 123–125
New England Commission of Higher Education, 3–4
North Carolina State University (NC State), 123–125
Northwest Commission on Colleges and Universities (NWCCU), 4, 6, 85

Obodaru, Otilia, 14
ongoing feedback, 15–16
online surveys, 121
open-ended items on surveys, 26, 78, 79–80, 121
open systems, 153
Organisation for Economic Co-operation and Development (OECD), 115–117
outcomes assessment, 42–43
outside vendors for evaluation instruments, 21–22

paired comparisons method of sorting, 45, 98
peers' evaluations, 46, 85
performance reviews, 7–11, 11–14. *See also* evaluations of administrators; evaluations of governing boards
Phillips, Ken, 23, 24
popularity contests, 11
portfolios for performance evaluations, 19–21, 37, 50
Predictive Learning Analytics, 23
professional evaluation firms, 49

rankings of successful results/behaviors, 44
rating scale on evaluation, 23–25
recognition of achievement, 64
red ocean strategy, 151–152
reflective statement of administrator/board, 20
regents, board of. *See* governing boards
results and intentions, 107
Rochester Institute of Technology (RIT), 92–94

SACSCOC (Southern Association of Colleges and Schools Commission on Colleges), 4–5, 6, 70, 85
salary adjustments, 15, 17
satisfaction surveys, 9, 11
Satrix Solutions, 13
schedule for evaluation. *See* frequency of evaluations
security of evaluation forms, 14
Seldin, Peter, 19–21, 37
self-assessment culture, 154–155
self-evaluation, 4–5; of administrators, 45, 46, 50; of boards, 99, 104, 105–106; comparing to other stakeholder evaluations, 106–107; formative nature of, 86; as imperfect process, 86
Shilp Gravures (company), 118
Sidley Austin (law firm), 118
Simmons University evaluations, 2
Southeastern Louisiana University (SLU), 68–70
Southern Association of Colleges and Schools Commission on Colleges (SACSCOC), 4–5, 6, 70, 85
Southern University System, 73
South Puget Sound Community College (SPSCC), 90
stakeholders: in administrative evaluations, 62–64, 65, 66–68, 69, 70–71; consulting with, 122–123; knowing needs of, 153. *See also* 360-degree evaluations
statement of responsibilities, 20
State University of New York (SUNY), 66–68
St. Charles Community College, 35
steps in administrative evaluations: appraising performance against criteria for success, 51–52; collecting and analyzing information, 45–46, 50–51; comparing self-evaluation to stakeholder evaluation, 53; externally scanning process/instruments, 48–49; formative advice, 54–55, 56; identifying critical functions of position, 40–41; improving process for next time, 56; informing stakeholders, 55–56; paring duties down to a subset, 46–47; prioritizing successful results/

behaviors, 44; selecting supervisory subcommittee, 39–40; sharing expectations, 47–48; streamlining process, 57; successful performance described, 42–43; summative judgments, 52, 53–54
steps in board evaluations: action plan development, 108–109; collecting and analyzing information, 100–101, 103–104; comparing self-evaluation to stakeholder evaluation, 106–107; distinguishing board and member responsibilities, 95–96; externally scanning process/instruments, 102–103; identifying information sources, 99–100; improving process for next time, 110; informing stakeholders, 109–110; prioritizing successful results/behaviors, 98; ranking performance, 105–106; selecting supervisory subcommittee, 94–95; sharing expectations, 101–102; sharing recommendations, 107–108; successful performance described, 96–98
strategic alignment: about, 143–145; accountability culture and, 144–145, 154, 157; accreditation process and, 145, 156–158; coordinated goals in, 145; destination addiction, 152; evaluation as tool for planning, 149–152; key points, 159; questions that focus on evaluation, 153–155; readjusting priorities, 158; reasons for, 146–149; red ocean *versus* blue ocean strategy, 151–152; steps for, 155–157. *See also* accountability
strategic objectives, 34
student ratings of instruction, 8–9
subordinates' evaluations of administrators, 45, 46
summative judgment, 51–52, 53–54, 108, 110
SUNY (State University of New York), 66–68
supervision of evaluations: in administrative evaluations, 39–40; in board evaluations, 94–95; in corporate world, 117. *See also* institutional review board (IRB) approval process

survey topics in administrative evaluations: administration, 77–78; budgeting, 76–77; communication, 75–76; demographic information, 78–80; institutional environment, 76; key points, 82–83; leadership, 75; learning environment, 76; mentoring and evaluation, 78; open-ended items, 78, 79–80
survey topics in individual board member evaluations: board relations, 135; campus and community engagement, 134; institutional relations, 135–136; key points, 138–139; knowledge and development, 134–135; matching constituency's perspective to, 136; mission and vision, 134; open-ended items, 136
survey topics in whole board evaluations: board actions, 128; board development, 128–129; board logistics, 127; board organization, 126–127; campus and community engagement, 131–132; demographic information of respondents, 132–133; fiduciary responsibility, 130–131; institutional performance, 129–130; key points, 138–139; matching constituency's perspective to, 136; open-ended items, 132; selection/supervision of administrators, 129; vision and planning, 130

templates, 42–43, 97–98
Texas A&M University, 8
Texas Tech University, 9
Texas Women's University (TWU), 70–72
360-degree evaluations: about, 2–3; as formative, 17; of governing boards, 85, 99–100; reasons for, 109; self-evaluation as part of, 6
trustees, board of. *See* governing boards
TWU (Texas Women's University), 70–72

universal mutual evaluation. *See* 360-degree evaluations
University of Tennessee, 37–39

vice presidents, 69–70

visitors, board of. *See* governing boards

Washington, Revised Code of, 89–90
weekly check-ins, 16
Western Association of Schools and Colleges, 4
Who are we? question, 153

whole board evaluations. *See* governing boards; survey topics in whole board evaluations
Whom do we serve? question, 153
women, bias against, 17–18
women's leadership style, 14
Workhuman (company), 18

ABOUT THE AUTHOR

Jeffrey L. Buller is a senior partner in ATLAS: Academic Training, Leadership, and Assessment Services. He has served in administrative positions ranging from department chair to vice president for academic affairs at four very different institutions: Loras College, Georgia Southern University, Mary Baldwin College, and Florida Atlantic University. He is the author of twenty other books on education leadership, a textbook for first-year college students, and a book of essays on the music dramas of Richard Wagner. Dr. Buller has also written numerous articles on Greek and Latin literature, nineteenth- and twentieth-century opera, and college administration. From 2003–2005, he served as the principal English-language lecturer at the International Wagner Festival in Bayreuth, Germany. More recently, he has been active as a consultant to the Ministry of Education and many universities in Saudi Arabia, where he is helping to improve academic leadership across the kingdom. Along with Robert E. Cipriano, Dr. Buller works through ATLAS to provide leadership training and consultancy all over the world.

www.ingramcontent.com/pod-product-compliance
Lightning Source LLC
Chambersburg PA
CBHW030139240426
43672CB00005B/186